D0474499

perfect pitch

perfect pitch

4) dirt

EDITED BY
SIMON KUPER and
MARCELA MORA Y ARAUJO

HEADLINE

First published in 1999
by HEADLINE BOOK PUBLISHING

10 9 8 7 6 5 4 3 2 1

ISBN 0 7472 7511 4

Typeset by
Letterpart Limited, Reigate, Surrey

Printed and bound in Great Britain by
Clays Ltd, St Ives plc

HEADLINE BOOK PUBLISHING
A division of Hodder Headline PLC
338 Euston Road
London NW1 3BH

contents

acknowledgements

Thanks to Richard Adams, Gary Blumberg, Paddy Breathnach, Tomaso Capuano, Robert Chote, Giles Constable, Kevin Cummins, Leonie Gombrich, Arran Henderson, Simon and Martin Luke, Fiona McMorrough, Rana Mitter, Juan Mora y Araujo, Wolfgang Münchau, Matthijs van Nieuwkerk, Vivienne Schuster, Alex Skorecki and Michael Thompson-Noel, and to Ian Marshall and his colleagues at Headline.

Submissions to *Perfect Pitch* are welcome. These should be accompanied by a stamped, self-addressed envelope and sent to: The Editors, Perfect Pitch, c/o Headline Book Publishing, 338 Euston Road, London, NW1 3BH.

introduction

MARCELA MORA Y ARAUJO and
SIMON KUPER

'One must always keep, in some twist of the ear, a little dust from the vacant lot,' says Jorge Valdano in this issue, quoting Borocoto.

This issue contains, in the twists of its ears, the dust and dirt of many places. It has an American bias spanning the continent. As usual, this time with Valdano, we bring you the prose of a man who has played the game professionally himself. But we also have Emma Lindsey who discovers the mould for Jamaican football – the underdogs of 1998 – giving us the chance to prove that in *Perfect Pitch* at least it's the taking part that counts, not the result. Daniel Samper remembers the bizarre experiences he endured as a director of a football club in Colombia – a dirty job indeed – making his brother's old job as Colombian president seem like child's play. From Brazil we chose, instead of Ronaldo/Nike conspiracy theories, to bring you a fable told by Rita Lee, a pop star who made it big in the seventies and was still rocking during the 1998 World Cup.

Closer to home our writers get dirt on their hands. Eamonn Sweeney uncovers Punjabis, the IRA, and the game in Ireland. Simon Buckby does the same for New Labour and the game in England. Simon Inglis chokes on his curry when he discovers that the gardener, who is not into football at all, has childhood memories shaped by the same ball Valdano talks about. For the second time we've included a piece submitted by a reader, who revisits the lost time of his early years as a player, coached by a feisty priest. For the first time, Roddy Doyle writes for *Perfect Pitch*, observing his own children falling in love for the first time – with football of course.

Amy Raphael penetrates the defensive wall that George Graham has built around his own personal shrine. Hunter Davies profiles Igor Stimac, while Hugo Borst and Simon Kuper write about Ruud Gullit.

Because football didn't exist before 1992, when Nick Hornby started all this madness, we asked Lynne Truss to re-review *Fever Pitch* six years on in an attempt to draw some conclusions regarding the Invention of Football Literature.

There was a time before that, however, and we are proud to have found two examples from it of the literati flirting with the ball. Michel Platini is interviewed by Marguerite Duras who asks him, 'What is this game, demonic yet divine?' And best of all, we believe, is the short story by Adolfo Bioy Casares and Jorge Luis Borges, two of the best writers in the Spanish language. Borges was famous for his hatred of football and this little-known story is a gem; few people know it exists at all and we include it in this issue to pay homage to the great writer whose centenary it is this year.

Valdano's ability to write puts us all to shame, but Borges' capacity to understand the stuff that dreams are made of, particularly in light of his contempt for the game, results in *Esse Est Percipi*. D.J. Taylor has produced an excellent analysis of arguably the most ancient form of football literature: match programmes.

We hope to have once again found voices to tell stories you would not hear anywhere else. Top flight, professional, dirty writing at its best.

year of the bullock

RODDY DOYLE

Rory has always been a great man for the questions.

– Do children die sometimes?

– Is there something called God?

– Was there chocolate when you were a kid?

– Do you have a vagina?

He has thrilled and plagued me with them since he spoke his first word. (His first word, by the way, was 'miserable' and he was looking out at the weather from the back of the car when he said it.) But since January 1998, when he opened his first packet of Merlin Premier League stickers in Bewley's Café on Westmoreland Street, the questions have been changing.

– Does Dennis Wise chew gum?

– How many Premier League stickers would fit in the *Titanic*?

He got the book with the tail-end of a book token he was given at Christmas and I bought him six packets of the stickers, to get him going. Three packets open, he already had Patrik Berger and three Martin Bullocks. I stayed well back; I fought the temptation to lean forward and straighten the stickers before they were pressed into their places in the book. I watched him come to grips with alphabetical order and sticker numbers from 1 to 504. Robbie Earle, Phil Babb and two more Martin Bullocks later, he was hooked. For the next six months he carried the book everywhere, gathered the pennies for the next packet, filled two rooms of the house with columns of swaps. Seven Paul Warhursts, five Matt Elliotts.

– Look at all my swaps.

– What will you do with them? Asked his mother.

– Swap them, he said, too polite to let her know that it was the most stupid question he'd ever heard.

But he didn't swap them. He went to school with hundreds of them swaddled in elastic bands but he always brought them home. Three Carl Vearts, nine Justin Edinburghs, one Robbie Fowler.

He'd open the packet, careful not to rip the bigger team stickers inside. He'd hold them face-down and turn them over one by one.

– Got him, got him, haven't got him, got him.

Jason Euell, Craig Short, four Kevin Pressmans.

– How many times does Paul Ince blink?

– What's your seventh favourite Premier League club?

Burnley was the answer the last time I asked myself that question, when I was twelve. Rory's only seven but kids are growing up younger these days. Jack, Rory's five-year-old brother, doesn't ask as many questions; he knows that the answers will eventually roll up to him anyway. But even Jack, who unplugged the fridge because he couldn't hear the telly and didn't bother telling us until the smell had already let us know, even Jack had been bitten by the bug.

– And Roddy?

– Yes, love?

– Are Man United crap?

– Yes, love.

Kenny Cunningham, Richard Shaw, three Garry Flit-crofts. I watched Rory take command of the world. As the pages got thick with stickers and the book broke away from its staples, he soon knew which page to flick to before he read the name or number; a glance at the card was enough. Autoglass, no hair – Chelsea. One 2 One, confused – Everton. Ora, shy grin, looks very familiar – Martin Bullock.

– Got him, got him, got him.

Vinnie Jones, Gilles Grimandi, two John Salakos.

– Is Vinnie Jones in jail?

– Is Asprilla Irish?

Every night we went through the book, page by page, face by face. Jack joined us, got in under my arm and admired the filling pages.

– Oh, my Dod.

Rory is a Liverpool fan. Give us the boy and we'll give you the man, say the Jesuits, so I bought Jack and Rory Chelsea pyjamas before they could walk properly. But I was lazy. I bought them the jerseys; they toddled around with the name of a bad beer emblazoned across their chests. I thought that the products would be enough – wallpaper was next on my list, then duvet covers. But I underestimated the boys; I ignored their capacity for loyalty, their determination to build their own canoes and paddle them.

– I went to school a Chelsea fan and came home a Liverpool fan, says Rory. – It's a mystery.

He never has explained to me why he changed teams and I know: he never will. And I know this as well: when he came home and announced the news, I was politely being told to fuck off and mind my own business.

But Jack still wore his Chelsea jammies. I could still hope.

– Who do you follow, Jack?

– And Liverpool, he said. – But I hate the black player.

Luckily, I was sitting on his bed; I had nowhere to drop. Before I expelled my five-year-old son from the house for being a Nazi, I decided to give him one last chance.

I took the book from Rory and opened it at the Liverpool page. I put it on Jack's lap.

– Show me, Jack, I said.

He pointed.

– Him.

Roy Evans, in a black sweatshirt.

Just at that moment, I loved Roy Evans. And I've remained fond of him since. I was upset when he went.

– Got him, got him, got him, Hi Martin, haven't got him.

Temuri Ketsbaia, Steve Potts, Celestine Babayaro.

Somewhere in March Rory watched a live game from start to finish for the first time. And then he ran out to the garden to kick a ball. I watched him and my heart turned. He was growing so fast. After the joy of hammering a burst ball against a wall, the only surprises life had left for him were sex and Elvis. Then his voice in the window.

– Fowler! Yes!

He was commentating. Rory had become a man.

I brought him to London, to see Liverpool play Chelsea, no father should have to go through what I went through that afternoon: I watched my team demolish Liverpool, 4-1, while my son cried into my shirt. *Oh my mama told me – there'll be days like this.* Fuck off, Van Morrison. Too young to feel let down or angry at the synchronised dopes in the Liverpool defence, Rory confronted the essential human tragedy: you breathe in and out, and your team loses. At the end of the game a man patted Rory's shoulder and spoke to me.

– Poor little c'nt.

I nodded back; thanks.

He was still crying as we left Stamford Bridge and the rain started belting down on top of us as we walked down Fulham Road. Remember the good things, I told him. You saw Liverpool for the first time, you saw them score a goal.

– What was the best thing about the day? I asked him.

– Fowler getting off the bus.

I'd been half-hoping that a stroll through the Chelsea Megastore, on top of the result, would tempt Rory south; I'd half-expected him to announce his defection on our way through the rain. But the answer, when it came, didn't surprise me. The tears were gone now. Not for the first time, I felt myself in awe of Rory and I wondered if I was holding his hand or if, in fact, he was holding mine. I wondered at this tenacity, his unshakeability. He'd seen him clearly, before the game, Robbie Fowler, on crutches, carefully climbing down the steps of the Liverpool coach. Fowler is Rory's own hero, although for most of Rory's Liverpool supporting career Fowler hasn't played. He was injured from February 1998 to late September. Seven months. One twelfth of Rory's life. With the World Cup and Michael Owen's deification at its centre. But Rory remained resolute. Fowler was his. Fed by his videos and book – *Robert Bernard Fowler was born in the notoriously rough Toxteth area of Liverpool on 9 April 1975* – he waited for Fowler's return.

Now, like Fowler again, Rory is playing.

– I scored nearly a hat-trick.

– Two?

– One.

He scored his first o.g. last Sunday. Straight after half-time, he put the ball into the net of the goal he'd been attacking a few minutes earlier. He wasn't upset; he was even a little bit proud of it. Not remotely as proud, though, as he is of the muck he accumulates every Sunday morning during the course of the game. He shows me his filth in the car on the way home.

– Look.

His knees are in there somewhere, under enough soil to make him eligible for an EU agricultural grant.

– And look.

There's a streak across his forehead.

– I did a header. And look.

He lifts his arm; there's more muck right under there.

– Am I the first person to do an armpitter, ever?

– Probably.

– Are you positive?

– No.

– I'll need a shower.

– Yes.

He grins.

Three Gerry Taggarts, Philip Neville, Graham Fenton. It's been a wonderful year. Andy Booth, Stan Lazaridis, Dion Dublin. Captured forever in the Merlin Premier League '98 Official Sticker Collection. Every sticker, every smile and haircut is a moment in Rory's life, and mine. I flick through the book and I like all these men; I'm very grateful to them. Gary Charles, Alex Manninger, Ramon Vega. I regret the retirements, sackings, relegations. Mark Wright, Ruud Gullit, Attilio Lombardo. And I always stop at Page 17, one of the Barnsley pages. I linger at the top right-hand corner. Born: 5-3-75. Place: Derby. Height: 1.64M. Weight: 68KG. Squad No.: 14. Name: Martin Bullock. There'll always be a place for Martin in any team I select.

Roddy Doyle's All-Time Great Eleven

Yashin

Facchetti   McGrath   Moore   Maldini

Jairzinho   Socrates   Bullock   Best

Fowler   Doyle Jr

esse est percipi

JORGE LUIS BORGES and ADOLFO BIOY CASARES

As an old roamer of the neighbourhood of Núñez and thereabouts, I could not help noticing that the monumental River Plate Stadium no longer stood in its customary place. In consternation, I spoke about this to my friend Dr Gervasio Montenegro, the full-fledged member of the Argentine Academy of Letters, and in him I found the motor that put me on the track. At the time, his pen was compiling a sort of *Historical Survey of Argentine Journalism*, a truly noteworthy work at which his secretary was quite busy, and the routine research had accidentally led Montenegro to sniff out the crux of the matter. Shortly before nodding off, he sent me to a mutual friend, Tulio Savastano, president of the Abasto Juniors Soccer Club, to whose headquarters, situated in the Adamant Building on Corrientes Avenue near Pasteur Street, I hied.

This high-ranking executive still managed to keep fit and active despite the regimen of double dieting prescribed by his physician and neighbour, Dr Narbondo. A bit inflated by the latest victory of his team over the Canary Island All-Stars, Savastano expatiated at length between one maté and another, and he confided to me substantial details with reference to the question on the carpet. In spite of the fact that I kept reminding Savastano that we had, in yesteryear, been boyhood chums from around Agüero and the corner of Humahuaco, the grandeur of his office awed me and, trying to break the ice, I congratulated him on the negotiation of the game's final goal, which, notwithstanding Zarlenga and Parodi's pressing attack, centre-half Renovales booted in thanks to that historic pass of Musante's.

In acknowledgement of my support of the Abasto eleven, the great man gave his maté a posthumous slurp and said philosophically, like someone dreaming aloud, 'And to think it was me who invented those names.'

'Aliases?' I asked, mournful. 'Musante's name isn't Musante? Renovales isn't Renovales? Limardo isn't the real name of the idol acclaimed by the fans?'

Savastano's answer made my limbs go limp. 'What? You still believe in fans and idols?' he said. 'Where have you been living, don Domecq?'

At that moment, a uniformed office boy came in, looking like a fireman, and he whispered to Savastano that Ron Ferrabás wished a word with him.

'Ron Ferrabás, the mellow-voiced sportscaster?' I exclaimed. 'The sparkplug of Profumo Soap's after-dinner hour? Will these eyes of mine see him in person? Is it true that his name is Ferrabás?'

'Let him wait,' ordered Mr Savastano.

'Let him wait? Wouldn't it be better if I sacrificed myself and left?' I pleaded with heartfelt abnegation.

'Don't you dare,' answered Savastano. 'Arturo, tell Ferrabás to come in.'

What an entrance Ferrabás made – so natural! I was going to offer him my armchair, but Arturo, the fireman, dissuaded me with one of those little glances that are like a mass of polar air.

The voice of the president began deliberating. 'Ferrabás, I've spoken to De Filippo and Camargo. In the next match Abasto is beaten by two to one. It's a tough game but bear this in mind – don't fall back on that pass from Musante to Renovales. The fans know it by heart. I want imagination – imagination, understand? You may leave now.'

I screwed up my courage to venture a question. 'Am I to deduce that the score has been prearranged?'

Savastano literally tumbled me to the dust. 'There's no score, no teams, no matches,' he said. 'The stadiums have long since been condemned and are falling to pieces. Nowadays everything is staged on the television and radio. The bogus excitement of the sportscaster – hasn't it ever made you suspect that everything is humbug? The last time a soccer match was played in Buenos Aires was on 24 June 1937. From that exact moment, soccer, along with the whole gamut of sports, belongs to the genre of the drama, performed by a single man in a booth or by actors in jerseys before the TV cameras.'

'Sir, who invented the thing?' I made bold to ask.

'Nobody knows. You may as well ask who first thought of the inauguration of schools or the showy visits of crowned heads. These things don't exist outside the recording studios and newspaper offices. Rest assured, Domecq, mass publicity is the trademark of modern times.'

'And what about the conquest of space?' I groaned.

'It's not a local programme, it's a Yankee-Soviet co-production. A praiseworthy advance, let's not deny it, of the spectacle of science.'

'Mr President, you're scaring me,' I mumbled, without regard to hierarchy. 'Do you mean to tell me that out there in the world nothing is happening?'

'Very little,' he answered with his English phlegm. 'What I don't understand is your fear. Mankind is at home, sitting back with ease, attentive to the screen or the sportscaster, if not the yellow press. What more do you want, Domecq? It's the great march of time, the rising tide of progress.'

'And if the bubble bursts?' I barely managed to utter.

'It won't,' he said, reassuringly.

'Just in case, I'll be silent as the tomb,' I promised. 'I swear it by my personal loyalty – to the team, to you, to Limardo, to Renovales.'

'Say whatever you like, nobody would believe you.'

The telephone rang. The president picked up the receiver and, finding his other hand free, he waved it, indicating the door.

Translated by Norman Thomas di Giovanni.

george graham: arsenal fan

AMY RAPHAEL

Croatia are about to knock Germany out of France 98, but I find myself more interested in the woman next to me. She is standing on her plastic seat, dancing. It is half-time and the woman, somewhere in her late fifties, has won two tickets to a World Cup game at the Stade Gerland in Lyon. She has brought a girlfriend along with her and they are having a brilliant time, dancing the Macarena. I am intrigued by the woman not because of her age or spectacular rhythm, but because during the first forty-five minutes she watched the players avidly, telling her friend how she would be informing Mr Graham all about them when she returned home.

Towards the end of the second half, we start talking. Maureen introduces herself and explains that she works at Leeds, as secretary to George Graham. I in turn tell her I am a journalist and her face lights up. 'You *must* interview Mr Graham,' she says, clutching my arm. 'He is such a good manager and a nice man.' She scribbles her number on a ticket stub and presses it in my hand, making me promise to ring.

I am not an Arsenal fan, but I have always had a certain curiosity about George Graham's Hampstead flat. Here, legend has it, he lives in an Arsenal shrine with a club badge fashioned out of mosaics in the back garden. And tulips planted in 4-4-2 formation. So I phone Maureen at Elland Road. We reminisce a little about the World Cup. She still can't quite believe that she went; I can't believe I sat next to her. She has already mentioned me to Mr Graham. He is interested in doing an interview. She suggests a trip to Leeds; I say London would be better. Hampstead better still.

After several phone calls, mild panic sets in: there is talk of Graham leaving Leeds. As the talk points to a move to Tottenham, I think little of it. The man who won the Double as an Arsenal player in 1971, and who, as manager, brought eight major trophies to the club, could never go to White Hart Lane. Could he?

In 1995, Arsenal fans were stunned when George Graham was sacked for 'keeping' £425,000 from their beloved club.

In November 1998, he stunned them again by announcing that he did indeed intend to move to Tottenham Hotspur. Again, they felt betrayed; he, by contrast, said he was facing his biggest challenge yet.

I am now even more curious about Graham's Arsenal shrine: here is a man who claims to be a fan, yet appears to show no understanding of how a fan's mind works. There are few people on the business side of the game who could be called fans, but perhaps George Graham is one.

Maureen is all tearful on the phone. She is worried about who her new boss might be, but also she is going to miss Mr Graham. Despite her concern, she forwards my correspondence with Graham to Tottenham.

I agree with Graham's new secretary to meet him at

Spurs Lodge, the team's Essex training ground. The possibility of visiting the Hampstead museum is becoming more remote each day.

George Graham – dour Scotsman; disciplinarian; creator of boring, boring football – is half an hour late. I sit outside his office and watch players return from training. Darren Anderton with a surprisingly healthy glow, David Ginola looking pleased with himself. Finally, Mr Graham arrives. He extends a hand, gives a firm, dry shake and ushers me into his office. He is, of course, immaculately dressed: brown cords, grey shirt, beige waistcoat and black shoes polished to catch the light.

The office could be at any club. There is nothing on the walls. His desk gives little more away: a copy of *World Soccer* and *News of the World*; a Dolce & Gabbana glasses case; a mobile phone and briefcase (which, I later discover, is full of handwritten notes and signed pictures of himself, in Leeds training kit).

'Have you been offered a cup of tea? No? That's a disgrace!' He asks his secretary to bring two teas.

I ask how he is and he smiles. 'Very well. Very well. It's good when your hobby is also your job – it can't be bad. Life's very good. I was happy at Leeds; Leeds was fabulous. However, my personal life was taking a bit of a beating. My fiancée lives down here in London, so I was travelling up and down the motorway every weekend. But I was quite proud of what I achieved at Leeds. I revamped the players' side and left it on a very, very good level. But this – Tottenham – is another challenge. And if there is one thing I do like, it's a challenge.'

It seems a little early to ask direct questions – and I

am wary of talking too soon about the fact that Graham was found guilty by the FA commission of accepting £425,000 from the Norwegian agent Rune Hauge as a 'gift' and therefore banned from football for a year – but I ask if it was a tough choice, leaving Leeds to take up the job at Tottenham.

'No, but only because of the personal situation,' he says, sipping his tea and then putting it carefully back on its coaster. 'After getting the sack at Arsenal, I thought I had better start to get my priorities right. I had always put my job way, way before my personal life but in 1995, I began to realise family and personal life is just as important as the job.'

In his year 'off', however, Graham did not only spend quality time with his family. He couldn't, of course, stay away from football. He appeared not only on BBC Radio and on Sky Sports, but also on Channel 4's *Football Italia*. It wasn't simply a matter of watching games; banned from working as manager anywhere in the world, George Graham had to manage the teams in his head. One side in the first half, the other in the second half. 'I would see if I could improve them,' he says, smiling, as much to himself as to me. 'It was good. It did me good.'

Appearing on *Football Italia* not only kept Graham's coaching skills up to scratch, but also gave him a rare opportunity to watch a team he loved. 'I've always been a big fan of AC Milan. What's that little guy called? The one at Atlético Madrid now? Oh yes, Arrigo Sacchi. Well, when he left Milan, Fabio Capello came back, it was probably the worst thing he [Capello] ever did. He won the Championship with Real Madrid and then came back to Milan, who had a poor team. He thought he could resurrect it, but it didn't work. So he only lasted one season. Success always comes to an end; look at Liverpool. Both teams have to rebuild. And both teams will be successful again.'

Graham loves the word 'success'. Alongside 'winning' and 'challenge'. This is why he fell in love with Arsenal; after winning nothing as a player at Chelsea, he went on to win trophies at Highbury. He says the idea of winning – at any club – motivates him, keeps him young.

A few days earlier, in a much-hyped game, Tottenham had drawn 0-0 with Arsenal at Highbury. Graham had returned to Highbury three times as manager of Leeds, but it was his first time with Tottenham. While the Arsenal fans booed him, he was shown on *Match of the Day* winking at a steward and looking oddly pleased with himself. 'That was just a bit of acting,' he attempts to explain. 'You should never let people think they've got the better of you. Never. That's why I always smile.'

What of the Arsenal fans? What of club loyalty? I tell him that before the game, I went in the Wig & Gown, a pub on Holloway Road, where I overheard an Arsenal fan say: 'Georgie's a fucking spiv. But he built this club, man. He fucking did. But he's going to get it today. 3-0.' He ignores the 'spiv' description and gives a stock answer – almost as though he is addressing a press conference.

'I can understand the fans. But I think this hatred between clubs is sad. Can't you support one team without hating another? When I was a little boy, I used to support a team called The Airdrieonians – from Airdrie. I was never a fan of either Glasgow Rangers or Glasgow Celtic, but I used to go and watch them as well . . . It was nice to go back to Highbury and get a result. It would've been more satisfactory to win 1-0, but I was happy with 0-0. After all,' he says with a smile, 'I've coached both defences.'

His mobile rings and he switches it off without answering it. Minutes later, the phone rings. Wrong number. It rings again straight away. The caller puts the phone down without saying anything. Graham grimaces. He is obviously irritated by both the stupidity and the lack of manners. He does not suffer fools gladly. This is his reputation: tough, intolerant. Yet he obviously has a three-dimensional character.

He warms up a little when I ask about the great lineage of Scottish managers. 'I have thought about it, of course,' he says. 'Matt Busby and Jock Stein both came from the same mining town. Bill Shankly came from a little Ayrshire community – again, a mining community. And then Ferguson and Dalglish came from Glasgow . . . and I'm from Bargeddie, a small village outside Glasgow. It is said that Scottish managers have a wonderful record, but I really haven't got a clue as to why. All I can think is that we are a passionate race.'

Graham pauses to reflect: this is his first considered answer. 'I noticed a few years ago that if you look at the history of trade unions, there is often a Scotsman in charge during major disputes. The Scots love a challenge, a battle; they are passionate about it . . . look at Gordon Strachan: he looks as though he could be another big-time manager. He's got the passion all right.' Graham suddenly, unexpectedly, laughs. 'Whether he'll have a heart attack or see it through, I don't know.'

If Tottenham win the Double, would Graham consider becoming manager of Scotland? He doesn't seem to notice that currently, the suggestion of such success for

Spurs is a preposterous notion. 'I really don't know. I love the day-to-day involvement. I think I must be a control freak because I love controlling the whole situation at a club. Anyway, I'm only fifty-three, I'm too young. And the pressure of pleasing everyone; all that media, all those journalists.'

Surely that applies at club level too? Graham insists he stopped reading the papers a long time ago. I point at the *News of the World*. 'I've only got that because a player has had a go at me in it. It's simply a reference point because I'm taking disciplinary action. I don't let anybody within my own club criticise me – if anyone has a problem, they should come to me instead of telling some journalist.'

Most fans would agree that Premier League players are over-paid, especially if they play sloppy football and bitch about their managers in the tabloids. George Graham is not sure what he thinks. When Sky first introduced live games, he was 100 per cent against it. Like many fans, he was convinced it would turn season ticket holders into armchair fans – now he admits he has been proved wrong. He talks of our stadia rivalling those in Italy and Spain and of the influx of foreign players.

Graham doesn't believe that players' wages should be capped, as long as big clubs such as Arsenal and Manchester United have a tacit agreement not to go over a certain weekly wage. But the higher the players' wages, the pricier the season tickets. How much, for example, are they at Tottenham? Graham has perhaps forgotten what it's like to be a paying fan. He looks blank. He is clearly irritated with himself for not being informed. 'I don't know. I think Chelsea's are the most expensive and then it's probably between Tottenham and Arsenal. David Pleat is the one to ask.'

Going to Stamford Bridge is about as affordable as going to the opera, I suggest, exaggerating slightly to provoke a response. 'That's ridiculous,' says Graham, his voice raised. 'You may be able to go to the opera twice a year, but you should be able to go to football every week. I don't know the answer to that one, but I see your point. We're starting to turn away people from White Hart Lane now. If I push Tottenham up into the top six, it will be even harder to get tickets.' He smiles at his vision of success. 'Then the value of the club will increase and be worth as much as, say, Arsenal.'

A good time to buy shares, then? 'Yeah, if I can get it right. I'll probably buy a few myself. Ha ha.' He looks serious again. 'Any more questions?'

I carefully suggest meeting up again, perhaps in Hampstead. He looks at me. 'I think the Arsenal memorabilia thing's been done before, don't you? I'm about to move from my flat to a house round the corner, and so obviously everything is going into storage.' I look worried; he winks. 'Hopefully then I will be able to start a Tottenham collection.'

You're a little fickle, I say, smiling. 'Christ can you imagine? A couple of hundred yards round the corner from his Arsenal memorabilia place, the new manager at White Hart Lane has a Tottenham collection. Anyway, I'm busy next week – it's the AGM – but perhaps we can meet again the following week.' He looks intently at his watch. I leave.

The mini-cab driver who picks me up at Spurs Lodge has

an Arsenal badge stuck on his dashboard. He asks what George Graham was like. I pause. 'Professional.' I don't know what else to say. Graham has been in football for almost forty years and knows how to deal with the press. 'Yeah, well,' says the cabbie. 'He's into all that discipline stuff, innit?'

The day after his fifty-fourth birthday and the day before Tottenham play Manchester United in the Worthington Cup, I am invited to George Graham's home. I am not sure if it is the Arsenal flat or the Tottenham house. When I arrive it is an apartment block and I am hopeful. No one answers the bell, so I stand in the bitter cold for eight minutes until a silver BMW turns into the drive and the horn is sounded.

Graham parks his car in the garage and emerges whistling. He is apparently in a good mood, but despises lateness and spends a few minutes explaining how he was caught out by a certain road being shut. The flat is on the ground floor and all the doors are shut. Graham opens the living room to reveal a pink and beige palace with a view of the garden. On one wall are a few cabinets displaying trophies and photos.

On each of the several occasional tables are magazines: *House & Garden*; *Country Living*; a Laura Ashley catalogue. They are neatly displayed as though in a hotel foyer. A series of paintings showing black and white abstract images of naked women adorns the walls.

I take off my coat and before I can say a word, Graham opens one of the closed doors. It is a small room with no natural light. It is the Arsenal museum. He looks at me and smiles. Radiating pride, he points at the black and white cigarette cards which date back to the Woolwich Arsenal days, to a cartoon strip with a character called Red Shirt, which ran in 1904. He explains that over the years people have offered him Arsenal memorabilia – someone once sold him a turn-of-the-century film upon which old players demonstrated various techniques. He spent time finding someone who could make black and white prints from the faint images.

On the opposite wall are images which involve Graham himself: a photo of the 1971 Double-winning side; a picture of him bursting with pride, carrying the '89 Championship trophy, with the sign 'This Is Anfield' in the background; signed cigarette cards of the players who won the Double under his management. He points at an oil painting of Thomas scoring that vital goal against Liverpool and says he recently had it reframed.

A shelf running round the top of the room holds dozens of bottles of ancient whiskies, which he also collects. On a bookcase next to the door are football books, old and new. Perfect copies of the early 20th century football bible, *Association Football & The Men Who Made It*, sit alongside biographies by modern players.

Graham points to Tony Adams' book, *Addicted*, which sits on his desk. 'I ask all the players I've worked with for signed copies of their books. I'm still waiting for Ian Wright to give me another copy of *Mr Wright*, because I mislaid the first one.' Leading me out, Graham apologises for not being able to show me his FA Cup medals, explaining they are in storage 'for safekeeping'.

While he boils the kettle, I go back to the living room. He shouts through that there is no fresh milk and asks if powdered will do. I say I take my coffee black. I look beyond the conservatory to the patio and there is no mosaic of the Arsenal badge. Graham brings in the drinks. He sees me peering into his back garden and smiles. 'There has never been a badge out there,' he says, without prompting. 'I don't know who came up with that.' And the tulips? 'I'd have a laugh occasionally by saying that. And not just 4-4-2 but also 3-5-2. He he he,' he giggles.

George Graham having a laugh? 'I'd say it in interviews to lighten things up a bit. I am well aware that I have this image of walking around with a big stick, a big whip and it's just nonsense. I will always be tagged as Saddam Hussein or whatever it was the press used to give me as a nickname, but I am simply *very* professional. Probably even ten years ago that sort of joking around would've been frowned upon. Successful managers are strong managers. Especially nowadays when players can turn round and say: Who cares, we're earning a fortune. Which isn't to say that I'm serious all the time.'

It suits the press to portray him as a dour disciplinarian, but look back at Graham's playing days, and it is evident that he has always had a mischievous and spirited side to him. He tells me one of his favourite stories. After playing together at Chelsea in the early sixties, George Graham and Terry Venables parted company, with Graham going to Arsenal and Venables to Spurs. Venables had a friend, Morris Keston, a Spurs supporter. Keston would often run into Graham, especially before Spurs were due to play Arsenal.

Graham's eyes sparkle as he remembers. 'Morris became convinced that every time he saw me before a derby game, Arsenal would win. So I made a point of trying to see him before each derby. One day, I tried to arrange to meet him but he refused. I decided to go to his flat, which was just behind Selfridges, in a lovely square. His wife opened the door and I could see Morris running down the hall. He locked himself in the bathroom. I'll never forget, it was really funny. I whispered to his wife, "Get me a chair," because above the bathroom was this little window. I quietly stood on the chair and tapped on the window. Morris looked up to see me standing there – and we won again the next day.'

More unexpected than George being King of Comedy is the fact that he almost became a pub landlord. As a player he had been reasonable but not outstanding; he used to joke about being mentally agile but lacking pace; in turn he was nicknamed 'Stroller'. He says Liam Brady and Glenn Hoddle are true examples of 'magnificent midfielders' and that Peter Osgood was the best nineteen-year-old he has ever seen, but Graham . . . well, he would never have picked himself.

After success at Arsenal, Graham went to Crystal Palace to play under Venables. He broke his leg. While he was recovering, Venables asked what he was thinking of doing when he retired. Graham had been helping Frank McLintock out at one of his pubs, learning the trade so that he would be ready to take on a tenancy of his own. Venables was not impressed. He convinced Graham to coach Palace's youth team: if he hated it, there was no obligation.

Within a month, Graham was hooked. 'I thought I was the last person in the world who would succumb to coaching,' he says, straightening an already straight pink cushion. 'I'd worked with some excellent coaches, from

Dave Sexton to Don Howe – who was a big influence on me – to Bertie Mee and, of course, Terry Venables. I thought there was no way I'd be able to touch any of their standards, but I worked at Palace for two-and-a-half years and absolutely loved it.'

Graham moved with Venables from Palace to QPR, and, after five years, decided he would try first team management at Millwall. When he joined the club, he didn't even negotiate a salary. He simply said: 'When I'm successful, I'll be expensive.' He accepted the £20,000 annual salary offered to him because it was double what he had been paid for five years at Crystal Palace and QPR. 'When Arsenal came for me, they were surprised at how much money I was on!' Graham smiles.

With Arsenal, of course, he was accused of creating boring, boring football but he won titles for the club (two League Cups, two Championships, the FA Cup and the European Cup-Winners' Cup, in less than a decade). He learned to trust his instinct and to have no regrets. He knew, for example, that he was right to sell Andy Cole to Bristol City for £500,000 plus a percentage: he only played one first team game, and when he was sold on to Newcastle, Arsenal made a further £900,000.

Instead of Cole, Graham played Ian Wright, a record signing of £2.5 million from Crystal Palace. 'That was a lovely one,' says Graham with a grin as cheeky as Wright's. 'He was a great signing ... I saw him on Saturday [when Spurs played West Ham] and he was as good as gold. I got on very well with Ian.'

Building an average team with a great defence, Graham was assured of a place next to Herbert Chapman, whose bust sits in the marble halls of Highbury as a tribute to his legendary management in the thirties. Until, that is, he accepted the £425,000 from Rune Hauge. It is time to ask. Why?

'When I left, I said the only bust of me to be put next to Herbert Chapman would be made of papier mâché,' he laughs. 'It certainly wouldn't be bronze.'

Seriously, you must regret making such an apparently basic mistake?

He looks cold for the first time today. 'But what is the point of looking back on it? What is the point?'

To understand. You loved Arsenal. You live in a flat with a shrine to the club.

'There's no point,' he begins again. 'OK. It was a downright mistake. A mistake. My career hit rock bottom. I had a decision to make. To walk away with my tail between my legs or to decide to come back. Everyone gets knocks in their life, but the winners are the ones who refuse to give up, to give in. And I made the decision to come back into management at the highest level; I was offered a job at Manchester City, but I just didn't think it was right. I came back with Leeds and I'm proud. It was fantastic what I did there, I tell you. And I've left them in a great condition. And whatever anyone says, I am one of the great Arsenal managers.'

He looks at me, deadly serious. 'As I say, there is no point in looking back on life. I can sit in that room and it brings back memories, but as soon as I close the door again, it's finished. I want more photos and trophies, and I think I will achieve more, too.'

At five o'clock each Saturday, Graham listens for Arsenal's results ('obviously, because of what I did there') but he also registers how Leeds have done. This season, however, his heart is at White Hart Lane. I thought he was joking when he told me at Spurs Lodge that he was thinking about starting a Tottenham collection. Apparently not.

'Why shouldn't I? I like to integrate myself with my job, wherever it is. I don't know what makes people successful, but I want everybody who works with me to integrate themselves too. I'm not against people having fun, I want them to enjoy their jobs, but only if they care about the consequences. I do believe in star players, but not at the training ground; there, everyone is equal, whatever may be written on their contracts. I don't want players turning up half-way through training and casually saying they were caught in traffic. It's not good enough. I want them to worry if they are late.'

He fiddles with a cushion before swearing for the first time. 'I want them to think, "Fucking hell, the boss is going to go berserk again." You hear some of the United lads, they still talk about Alex Ferguson like that. It's not even awe, it's fear, and that's how it should be. So far, the boys at Tottenham have been superb with me. I tell you, they want to win.'

As well as reading American sports psychology books in bed, Graham firmly belongs to the European school of football management which puts emphasis on diet and discipline. He thinks footballers earn executive salaries and should therefore behave like executives. Footballers like to have a figurehead, they need direction. 'They shouldn't be going out getting pissed on a Thursday night. Because they've only got a short career. Maybe Liverpool were an exception when they had better players – in the days of Dalglish and Hansen – but in my opinion they can't get away with it now. None of this crap of the last five years, the Spice Boys and so on. It's great if you're winning, but embarrassing if you're not. I should know; we recently beat them 3-0 at Anfield in the Worthington Cup.'

The phone rings; he starts talking about team line-ups for tomorrow night's game against Man United, then decides better of it and says he'll call back later. 'Football is no longer just a sport; it's a business. It's a profession. Everyone talks about diet now, about banning alcohol from the players' hotel rooms and insisting on them drinking still water before and after the game. Which isn't to say you can't have fun, just don't go to a nightclub where everyone knows you, act like an idiot and then be surprised the next day when you're on the front page of every newspaper.'

I have brought two things to show Graham. The first is a catalogue for a sale of football memorabilia at Christies in Glasgow. In it there are a number of rare Arsenal items, including a 1974 painting by Yates Wilson showing Tom Whittaker giving a team talk five minutes before kick-off. Graham recognises the painting immediately and reads the accompanying description out loud. He then finds an FA Cup winners' medal from 1910. 'The lovely thing about the FA Cup medal is that it has never changed. In my Arsenal days, I tried to buy Alex James' medal. I offered 1,500 quid and it went for 5,000. The PFA bought it, so at least it's still in football.'

The second is a copy of *Goal* from 3 October 1970. On the front is a photo of George Graham in an Arsenal shirt.

Inside, there is a description of Graham which suggests he was being a little modest when he had talked about his playing: 'His influence on the team has been outstanding. His brilliant control, inch-perfect passing and darting raids down the middle have caused havoc time and again . . . he didn't always look worthy of the [£75,000] fee. His sometimes petulant performances had the fans exasperated, but all has been forgiven.'

Graham, however, ignores the glowing review. 'Jesus, 1970 and I've got some hair. I've got hundreds and hundreds of photos from this period.' He spots a photo of Billy Bremner. 'Amazing. That was a great Leeds team. It's a good side now, just a couple of players short, but they've got some first-rate youngsters. The boy Woodgate, he's fantastic.' Here is George Graham as fan-manager, almost unable to believe that he has had the chance to work with such great clubs – it is strange to watch his childish enthusiasm, given that he normally takes his work and achievements easily in his stride.

Enthused by the memories evoked by *Goal*, Graham gets off the sofa to show me the contents of the cabinets. There's a photo of Graham with Alex Ferguson – 'we caught him smiling!' – and another of Graham with Terry Venables. There's a Footballer of the Week trophy awarded by the *Daily Mail* in 1970 and a plate for Divisional Manager of the Month 85-86; Graham says it used to be a bottle of champagne until he asked for something a little more permanent. 'These days you get Carling No 1 Manager of the Month, which is an awful, ugly trophy.'

Among the memories of his footballing career is a photo of Graham as a sulky-looking baby ('some would say I haven't changed') and dozens of photos of his son and daughter. He says his daughter, a school teacher on maternity leave, is a football fan – of whichever team he manages. His son, however, is not that interested, not wanting to live in his father's shadow (which makes the fact that he is brutally attacked in a pub less than forty-eight hours later by a drunken Arsenal fan for his father's betrayal of the club all the more senseless).

Tomorrow evening Tottenham will play Manchester United in the Worthington Cup. As Graham discusses the game, he leans back into the sofa and spreads his arms expansively across the top. He is, he says, relaxed. Tomorrow the team will go for lunch at a hotel and have a sleep in the afternoon. Graham will join them for a team talk just before the game. He will be wearing a smart suit; he thinks it's a silly pretence to wear a tracksuit unless you've just been training with the team.

'I think Spurs – the club, the fans – need a lift now, to tide them over while I'm rebuilding. I won't kid anybody. This is a big job. But even if we do beat Manchester United's so-called reserves – that's a bit of a laugh, with internationals such as Sheringham, Giggs, Berg, Johnsen and Butt; I know their team, anyway – we've got a long way to go. We need quality. Real quality.'

The door bell rings and Graham excuses himself, picking up a video on his way. 'Somebody asked me to make a video for his son's bar mitzvah,' he explains. The man at the door, who is possibly a neighbour, sounds very appreciative and offers to give some money to the charity of Graham's choice.

'No, no,' says Graham firmly. 'Thank you very much.'

He deftly changes the subject. 'I was playing tennis the other day with Susan, my fiancée . . .' The man listens. Graham is keen to go. 'I hope the bar mitzvah goes well. No, no, it's been a pleasure. Bye now.'

He whistles as he walks back to the living room. I ask him if making videos for bar mitzvahs is part of the deal of being manager at Tottenham.

George Graham winks. 'Whatever it takes. Whatever it takes.'

will adrian pop the question?: the sociology of the soccer programme

Not long ago I was engaged on one of those domestic duties that us thirtysomething fathers-of-two so proudly undertake – giving the children a bath – when a blundered-into carrier bag tipped over and spilled its contents out across the floor. It contained the following items: a) several copies of an unusually pretentious student magazine I used to co-edit (sample article: 'The Post-Structuralist as Boddhisittva'), b) a Christmas card from a schoolfriend named John Atkins whom I haven't seen since 1976, c) a photograph of myself aged seventeen in cross-gartered stockings and a tea-cosy hat playing Malvolio in *Twelfth Night*, and d) a copy of the match-day programme for the Norwich City versus Millwall Division Two game of 12 February 1972. No bets accepted on which of these souvenirs of past life caught my eye, or how I decided to spend the next five minutes. As the noise from the bath grew more insistent ('But he has got my duck!' 'Shut up Benjy, you old poo!') and the queries from downstairs more, well, querulous ('Isn't it time . . .' etc etc) I browsed on. Curiously, the memories prompted by this flimsy six-by-four booklet of a quarter of a century ago weren't particularly exact – although I remember the circumstances and the result (a top-of-the-table stand-off that ended 2-2) I've an idea that my dad, fearing crowd trouble (then, as now, the Millwall hordes were the most gentlemanly of visitors), wouldn't let me go. No, in rediscovering a pair of team-lists that included Kevin Keelan and Doug Livermore, Eamonn Dunphy and Harry Cripps I was roaming not merely through a mediocre football match from the early seventies (we got promoted by the way, they didn't) but through an entire lost world.

Light reading takes various forms, of course. George Orwell once volunteered that, last thing at night or in the minutes while your bath filled up, there was nothing to beat a bound volume of the *Girl's Own Paper*. One of the best stories in circulation about Iris Murdoch and her husband John Bayley concerns the weekend hostess who early one morning decided to take the then newly married couple a cup of tea. Murdoch was sitting bolt upright in bed in her nightdress poring over a German grammar. Bayley was similarly absorbed in a copy of *Woman's Realm*. Personally I'd settle for a stack of *Look and Learn*, a children's paper that my parents used to buy me in the pre-teen years. The average soccer programme fits squarely into this category – a wafer of sociological litmus-paper, full of queer detail about past time, the attitudes and assumptions that infect not simply our national game but the life lived out alongside it. Any social historian worth his salt who wanted to discover what English life was like in, say, the period 1966-79, that crucial World-Cup-to-Thatcher span, could do worse than assemble a couple of hundred football programmes. At the same time, the historical fragments they offer are that much more interesting for being unselfconsciously expressed. Asked to pronounce about their past experiences, most people turn formal and reductive. Asked to drone on about football, on the other hand, they immediately drone on about football, thereby letting all kinds of cats out of the socio-historical Umbro bag.

On the desk before me lies a small pile of Norwich City FC programmes. Chronologically, the selection ranges from 1972 to 1998 (in fact the pile starts with the Norwich/Ipswich game of 1951 – in effect a typed list of names and a few ads, and thus useless for forensic purposes, although it's interesting to find that you could get a Norwich Building Society mortgage of four per cent in those days). Physically, it extends from the frail *aide-mémoire* of the Millwall game (although these early examples claim to include something called the 'Football League Review') to giant contemporary glossies full of colour pictures of Matt Jackson being stretchered off and brutish opposing defenders trying to stand on Darren Eadie's head. Never mind what it may tell us about Norwich City over the past twenty-five years (which might be summarised as 'We're doing our best here, but there isn't very much money and the talent keeps leaving'), what do they tell us about soccer in general and the wider patterns uncoiling behind it?

The first thing to be noted – the most obvious thing, perhaps, from the point of view of the punter – is that at some point in the late 1980s somebody decided that there was money to be made out of soccer programmes if you went about it in the right way, that is if you put the price up and relied on the loyalty of what is effectively a captive audience. In 1973 the glorified team-sheet that was the Norwich programme retailed at a modest 7p. Five years later, even with colour photography, it was only 20p. A decade on it was still under a pound, before re-emerging in late 1990s splendour at £2 a throw – that's right, more than the *New Statesman*. A quick look at the Mars Bar Index of retail price inflation – a failsafe way of marking down how prices have risen in real terms – soon establishes what a rip-off the average programme has become. In twenty-five years the price of a Mars Bar has risen approximately eight-fold (4p to 32p). The cost of the average football programme, on the other hand, has risen by a factor of twenty-eight.

Needless to say, various improvements have been taken in along the way. 'Design' came in at the end of the seventies; letterpress printing was gone a few years later; by the mid-eighties one has an impression of something semi-professional rather than a series of slips of paper forwarded to a two-room printer by the club secretary (as it happens the 1972 programme was printed by an outfit called the Modern Press, whose other credits included our church magazine). Undoubtedly, this incremental march of sophisticated know-how mirrored the broader sprint towards commercialisation for which most clubs began to limber up in the early eighties. In 1972 the masthead at the top of the opening inside page contains, in addition to chairman and directors, simply the names of the Manager, the Secretary, the Hon. Surgeon and the 'Hon. Medical Officer', and there is a single phone number. By 1984, though, the personnel is clearly expanding: there are commercial managers and physios to add to the recently created post of 'Club Medical Officer'. Come 1998, corporatism has struck: a three-inch-long roster of sales managers, corporate sales managers, directors of football, directors of the football academy, heads of security and so on. No reflection on the club's priorities, of course, that Bruce Rioch, the manager, comes a lowly twelfth in this table of precedence.

And yet amid all this corporate flag-waving, the underlying spirit of the enterprise seems much the same. This is particularly noticeable when you take a look at the advertisements with which soccer programmes are traditionally bulked out. In the early seventies these were starkly minimalist, almost like the spoof ads on shopfronts in *Viz* cartoons ('Smoke tabs/Eat bread' etc) not to mention casually sexist. 'Where do canaries take their birds?' Why, to a perch at the Eatanswill grillroom or somewhere. 'Does mum need a rest?' Then whisk her off to Pete's Pieshop. Until at least the mid-eighties the club promotions followed this line, with pictures of curvy 'City girl Donna', who needless to say was 'all kitted out and ready for action'. The early seventies programmes even have recruitment ads, along with the solicitors and sports shops, nearby pubs and the Chinese restaurants of the Prince of Wales Road. Move forward a quarter of a century and, again, the modern world has swept in – Ladbrokes, the Norwich and Peterborough Building Society, Worthington – and yet, curiously, what might be called the semiotics, the linguistic code that governs these exercises, is all but unchanged.

Fundamentally, adverts in soccer programmes consist of jaw-breakingly inept sporting puns. Thus: 'Make your goal the Mustard Pot – within shooting distance of this ground' (1972); 'Team up with NUNNS for new Ford and quality used cars' (1973). And how, twenty-five years later, do Custom Kitchens of Lowestoft seek to press their wares upon the public? Why, 'If your kitchen's past its best – kick it into touch.' Somehow there is something deeply reassuring about this sort of lame wordplay in among the ads for Canary websites and satellite crap – like finding out that Enoch Powell was kind to cats or that Will Self likes eating sherbet dabs – a tiny whiff of humanity stealing up among the smoking corporate chimneys.

Talk of humanity leads one inexorably to the playing staff. What might be called the personality angle came fairly late to the world of Norwich City programmes. The only player intelligence back in 1972 was a couple of terse paragraphs to the effect that City had acquired centre-half Bobby Bell on loan from Crystal Palace and that Albert Bennett – one of the first forwards ever to own a pair of white boots – was being forced into retirement by a chronic knee ailment. A year later this wall of reticence had broken down sufficiently to produce a brief enco-mium to new signings Mel Machin and John Benson (John Bond had just been appointed manager, which may have something to do with this unlooked-for transpar-ency) and a pat on the shoulder for promising reserve performers ('This young man who has been making folk sit up and take notice with his displays for Gorleston is at present on trial at Carrow Road' etc etc). The end of the seventies, though, brings the first glimmerings of that well-known sporting delusion – that what players do off the field is interesting: gossip from the changing-room, despatches from the field hospital next door (a physio-therapist's feature about the treatment of skin injuries is full of stern capitalised injunctions to use CLEAN HANDS and a STERILISED NEEDLE) and the usual witless player profiles. Kevin Bond, recently shoehorned into the side by his old dad, declares on his debut that 'For me it is going to be a special night, and one that I have been looking forward to for a long time'. Subsequently a note of brisk realism kicks in: 'It's going to be an absolute disaster if we don't win.'

Ah, those player profiles! In bland, horrifyingly furnished homes situated here and there across the county of Norfolk, side by side with Cheryl, Mandy and the kids, or solitary amid flaring carpets, City's finest smile grimly for the photographer and nervously gear up for his sidekick's questions. Those questions! Favourite car? Favourite TV show? Best match? Biggest ambition? What follows, year upon year, is the most fantastic display of cultural naffness imaginable outside an Alan Partridge half-hour. Thus John Deehan (1984) confesses to a liking for Crown Green bowls, admits that his favourite comedy act is Cannon and Ball and that he admires the musical skills of Billy Joel. Promising youngster Andy Fensome (1988) reveals, implausibly enough, that his nickname is 'Fenno', his chief superstition wearing a shin-pad on his left foot, his favourite reading the *Sun*, and his hobbies watching TV and listening to music. Naturally no one expects professional footballers to murmur about their copies of *A La Recherche du Temps Perdu* (' "I think the Kilmartin translation is immeasurably superior to the Scott-Moncrieff," says Mark "Toppo" Topham') but there is something faintly masochistic about this relentlessly advertised mundanity. One can see why the programme compilers have always been so keen on these evocations of Darren forking pizza with Sharon and the girls or Shane poring over the *Mirror*. Their ordinariness perfectly suits the average fan's expectations, leaves him, or her, with the comforting thought that Darryl, Chris or Kev is *exactly like us* . . . except that he happens to be able to play football. Even here, though, in one of the remaining bastions of the old-style game, comes evidence of sophistication, style, and of course *money*. 'Fenno' prattles on about his digs, the nice couple who look after him and the family dog. Nineteen-year-old Master Adrian Forbes (1998) has found the dosh from somewhere to buy his own house in Thorpe Marriot ('My Mum and Dad said you can't go wrong with bricks and mortar. I'm lucky enough to be in a position where I'm earning good money and the last thing I want to do is squander it. I'm just looking for a good investment.') where he spends time cooking for his 'student girlfriend Rachel'. His *student girlfriend Rachel*! I used to hang around the old Trowse training ground twenty-five years ago watching the apprentices practise, and let me tell you none of them would have been seen dead with a student girlfriend. Even so, you see, despite being black, which hardly anyone in Norfolk is, Adrian is still 'one of us' – saluting his good fortune, sending videos of himself back to his old granddad in St Kitts and relishing the 'good feeling around the club . . . The players are definitely working hard.'

The players have changed in other, no doubt sociologically significant ways, too – stopped being called Trevor and Ken and Ted and become Darren and Darryl and Jason, stopped wearing their hair like the men in the ads you still see in old-style barbers and gone through a gamut of styles ranging from down-market seventies pop star (bunch of grapes perm) to regulation late-nineties billiard ball. Still one of us, though, despite the Norfolk farmhouses and the flash cars, and still subject to the same linguistic makeovers, a structural code unchanged since its late-seventies infancy: 'the lads' (the playing staff); 'the backroom boys' (the non-playing staff); 'the unsung heroes' (groundsmen, tea-ladies etc); 'the stars of the future' (any minimally competent trainee). A whole guide-book could be written on the language of the soccer programme, its routine garnishes and evasions and the real meaning of its ritual phrasings. Thus:

'The club believes . . .'	*the chairman says*
'In the club's best interests'	*in the chairman's best interests*
'Versatile all-rounder'	*can't think where to play him*
'Veteran defender'	*on the way out, sadly*
'Early performances lacked consistency'	*bottom*
'Our lynx-eyed target-man'	*plays up front*
'Confident of retaining x for years to come'	
	bastard wants more money

But beneath this relentlessly applied language-anaesthetic can be glimpsed all kinds of incidental miseries and tragedies. What happened to Norwich's 'star of the future' Andrew Pearce (1982), a schoolboy goalie whose ambition was 'to succeed Chris Woods', the biggest influence on whose career was 'PE teacher Mr Bussell', and who showed a rare flash of taste in nominating David Bowie as his favourite singer? Disappeared in the world of park football and vanished glory, presumably. If it comes to that, I don't recall 'Fenno' making the first team. Or any other first team.

Turn to the first-page welcomes, usually by the manager, occasionally anonymous, and the language becomes hugely significant. The 'Carrow Road notebook' of early

1972 has all the effortless cliché one associates with these things ('Football has a habit of unsettling predictions . . . Revenge would be sweet') but the central metaphor comes straight from the Battle of the Somme: today's game is nothing more than the start of the final 'push' that will see us to promotion. Ron Saunders' manager's notes strike an almost Smilesian note of self-help: 'If we are to win today we are going to have to work very hard and EARN it.' In other words, if it rolls in off the defender's leg by accident we'd sooner not have the points, ta very much. Ten years later Kenny Brown is more concerned about 'entertainment' and, in the light of suspect home form, fulfilling obligations to the fans ('If there is one place we want to do well it is here in front of you.') Fifteen years further on, Bruce Rioch is stressing the virtues of resilience, hard work, effort, pulling together, while delivering many a keen-eyed insight into the nature of the game ('Supporters saw a completely different game to the Queens Park Rangers match and they have to be aware that these tight games can go against you if you're not careful.') Make no mistake, *this is a very serious business*.

Actually I find it very difficult to laugh at this kind of thing. Again, if you wanted to decode the attitudes *towards the game* expressed in any football programme in the past twenty-five years, they would go something like this:

A successful team gets to the top by hard work
Team spirit and loyalty are worth any amount of
prima donnas
Supporters come to be entertained
In the last resort it's a game
We're all ordinary blokes here

All exemplary Corinthian sentiments eh? And here, quaintly enough, the soccer programme, or at any rate the kind of soccer programme put under this admittedly partial microscope, declares itself as one of the great subversive influences at work in the modern game. Professional soccer, it scarcely needs saying, is awash with the money sharks, the corporate hoodlums, the Freddie Shepherds, for whom players are 'assets' and walking bank loans, and yet here, down at bedrock level in the only real channel of communication between club and fan, is a kind of oasis of decency, humility and good humour. To skim through the most recent Norwich City offering (a Worthington Cup tie against Wigan from September 1998) is to cry a little at the countless courtesies and politeness on offer – how the non-players mentioned are invariably given their 'Mr' or 'Mrs', how the band of Ghanaian schoolgirls who wrote in asking for pen-friends are described as 'these young ladies', and somebody hopes that the referee – sorry, 'the man in the middle' – 'enjoys his evening here at Carrow Road'. Even the Adrian Forbes interview wonders if the Caribbean holiday with Rachel will end with his popping the question. The contrast between the attitudes of the average boardroom and the queer, old-fashioned notions of solidarity, communal feeling on display in a publication like *On The Ball City* is hugely revealing. No doubt this is a selective analysis – and certainly such Chelsea programmes as I've seen give the impression of a highly unpleasant man lecturing a fairly unpleasant constituency – but the gap between the average soccer programme and the nastiness of the tabloids is still cheeringly wide. And if only for old time's sake, and to mark the continued existence of a world which despite the efforts of the *Sun* and the super-agents and Ken Bates is still not quite dead, a small part of me hopes that Adrian and Rachel make it to the altar.

D.J. Taylor's novel Trespass *will be published in May (Anchor, £6.99); his* Thackeray *will be published in October.*

what kind of a game is this – demonic and divine?

MARGUERITE DURAS (1914–1996)

'What kind of a game is this – demonic and divine?'
Marguerite Duras asks Michel Platini in the course of the
most incongruous, naïve and weird interview one could
ever envisage between the French football star and the no
less celebrated diva of French literature. It was in 1987,
when the two participants had reached the peak of their
respective careers: three times European Player of the
Year for him and the prix Goncourt for her (for *L'Amant*).

(. . .)

MD: Did football get you down?

MP: No, never. It was all that went with it that got me
down. Not the football.

MD: Can I call you a victim of football, that's to say of
your day-to-day life as a footballer?

MP: Football started as a passion. I always had that
passion. What got me down at a certain stage was going
here and there to play matches. That's what got me down.
I was sick and tired of it.

MD: What year did that start?

MP: From the moment I was on a downward curve.

MD: 1984?

MP: No, 1983 and 1984 were my best years. I'd say at
the end of 1985, when we won the intercontinental cup. I
was with Juventus and we were world club champions.

MD: Did Heysel come into it?

MP: Heysel was earlier. Four months earlier. In May 1985. And my peak was in December 1985. And after that . . .

MD: I can see an angelism in football. I find people, men, in the sense of humans, in a state of purity that cannot be stopped by anything and that greatly moves me. And I think that's what I chiefly feel when I watch football. Because I do watch football. I saw you in Mexico. It was Mexico, wasn't it? Yes, I saw you, I saw you suffer, I wanted to kill Maradona, too. You see I was fully functional.

MP: Chauvinism!

MD: No, although I think the notion of homeland is everywhere, including there. And I think the football nation takes the place of the land of one's birth. But do you agree with the word 'angelism'? Angelism has no frontiers, no homeland. I must tell you: but for you I shouldn't have found that word. Forget it . . .

MP: I forget it.

MD: The footballer is on totally exposed ground. He is unprotected. If he lies, it's obvious. If he's frightened, it's obvious. If he's a silly fool, it's obvious. If he's a little bastard, it's obvious.

MP: It's easy for football people to see it, it's difficult for others.

MD: I'm saying that it's obvious in the play, for you. But there are people who watch the players too. Women for example . . .

MP: For the really knowledgeable, it's obvious. Not necessarily for everyone. There are players who show off and don't work for the team. Because the aim, the ultimate purpose of football is to make the team win. It's not to win yourself.

MD: There are footballers who play to the gallery too. But the great thing is in fact solidarity with the team.

MP: That's true. There's the guy who's good but doesn't make the team good. He may be good; the team is not good. There are guys who are not good, who are criticised, but who make a team good. But it's odd that people like you, who are not part of the football world, should notice it. Because for us, we know. When you play, when you see, you know. But for the public, it's difficult to understand that in football.

MD: My job in the world is to watch. The football pitch is a place where the other guy is the same as you are. You're equals.

MP: Absolutely.

MD: It's unique. Think about it, it's unique. It's limitless, bottomless, it's terrifying.

MP: If you like.

MD: So that's what makes football so amazingly attractive. You say: 'You are dangerous, you can be very dangerous . . .'

MP: At the level of repercussions, you are dangerous. You can have worldwide repercussions. You aren't even aware of it.

MD: That's true. I read the number of deaths in your book. Since Lima [320 dead] it's like a wartime casualty list.

MP: You know, when you play with passion, you don't think of that. It's true we can be dangerous and we carry some weight in the world and we don't use it because we don't know about it. And I don't know if one has the right to use it.

MD: I was watching television when the events of May 1985 took place at Heysel. One didn't know what was happening. It was as if, all of a sudden, the nature of the world had changed, one no longer recognised its shape. The feeling one was going mad, one had that feeling, confronted with Heysel. You were there, weren't you?

MP: Yes, but I didn't experience it. I was in the changing rooms.

MD: We saw you walk past. You didn't look at anything. You didn't look at the camera.

MP: They asked us to go out and calm the young fans down a bit. We were the only ones. I mean the eleven Juventus players and the eleven Liverpool players. We were the only people who didn't see the drama. We were in the changing rooms, getting ready for the match. That means that what hundreds of millions of people saw, we didn't see.

MD: But in spite of the eighty people crushed, who were dead or dying, you played. That was the only way to limit the disaster, to stop it.

MP: I'll tell you one thing: in football the players have no power. They are given orders by the managers. And the managers made the decision to play in order to protect the surroundings. If we didn't play, there'd be a manhunt in Brussels.

MD: So let's get this right: what made them mad? What was it that really made them mad?

MP: They were already fanaticised by the football. What made them mad was that they heard – you know, in those huge arenas they hear all sorts of things, not necessarily correct – that the English had *killed* thirty-five

Italians. But they hadn't been *killed*. The dead at Heysel were crushed by people escaping over the wall that collapsed, but they weren't assassinated.

MD: That should be shouted from the rooftops: the Heysel dead were not assassinated.

MP: That's what made a section of the public mad. Because in the other part of the stadium, in the curve, no one knew what had happened. Like us, they completely forgot. In the first place, they hadn't seen the horror; the horror, it's as if you were told a plane had crashed, thirty-seven dead, 200 dead . . . You don't see anything. Right, afterwards you go and take a plane. And then, when you're on the football pitch, you think about the football, which is your passion, your youth, your adolescence, you can't think that there were thirty-five dead while you were playing. When I score a penalty I'm happy; when you get down to it, football lets me escape from human misery. I escape completely, I should say I *escaped* because I don't play any more. But it's true that you don't think of anything when you're playing football. That day I became a man! I moved from a world where football was a game to a world in which football became a kind of violence. That's to say, that at a certain time, you have children's toys. And then at a certain time you no longer have children's toys. Well, that day I no longer had children's toys. I had become a man.

MD: But you were still playing with dynamite. You have 80,000 people in a stadium. It's a tragic fact.

MP: *You* know it, but I didn't. Because my dream was to play football in front of as many people as possible, for football to be a spectacle, for people to be happy together to sing . . . Otherwise I always loathe the crowds. I've never been to the theatre, I've never been to the cinema.

MD: Yes, but then if you take an individual who finds it distressing, who is full of images, atrocious images, of war, invasions, camps and who can't bear to be close to the crowd. And at the same time he is alive. Because football, after all, is one of the great joys of the human race, one of the most obvious, the most complete. How do you experience that contradiction?

MP: I've never experienced it.

MD: You have never been frightened in a stadium?

MP: No. I was in the middle of the stadium, protected by wire fencing.

MD: And the 80,000 people?

MP: That's football.

MD: What kind of a game is this – demonic and divine?

MP: Football is loved. Why is it loved? I'll tell you why it's loved. Because it has no shred of truth. It has no truth. The strongest will never win against the weakest in football.

MD: Do use some word other than truth . . . No law?

MP: No law. In a collective sport, you have to be stronger in spite of *yourself*. It's not necessarily the one who wins who's the strongest. The French team achieved a certain level among the strongest. But afterwards . . . Then you remake the world. Why? Because, for example, a goalkeeper slipped and you lost 1-0. Then you will be explaining, hurling crap at the team, doing anything because the goalie slipped! It's not his fault. Perhaps he didn't have good studs. So football is made up of mistakes, because a perfect match is 0-0. If nobody makes any mistakes, it's 0-0. So there must necessarily be mistakes.

But no one knows why mistakes are made. So we explain football by the mistake of a goalkeeper or of some guy who botched his shot; instead of shooting there, the ball went over there and rolled under the keeper, you've won 1-0, you're world champions. That's the basis of football. There is no truth. That's why everyone loves football.

MD: You have to take mistakes into account, absurdities as well. The fellow who dives in a certain direction when he should have dived in another and he can't explain why. That makes me laugh till I cry.

MP: Absolutely, yes! It's a game that has no truth, no law, nothing. And people try to explain it. But nobody manages to. That's why you can always talk about football, write articles, etc.

MD: Can you go so far as to say there's a certain madness that takes possession of the players?

MP: Certainly. There's a madness that takes possession of the players at certain moments and not at others.

MD: You lose your head?

MP: You can lose your head, you can suddenly go and fire a ball at the referee. You can go and punch an opponent. Then you're playing with ten men and you lose the match! Or else you have a stroke of madness, but more like genius, and you go and make a supermove and you win 1-0 and you're world champions. But why, how can you know if you have to make that supermove just then, in the thirty-seventh minute? And why? That's football. Impossible to explain it.

MD: If those men were perfect, if the players were perfect, there wouldn't be any football?

MD: You'd have 0-0, there'd never be any goals. If nobody made a mistake it would always be 0-0.

MD: But horses in races don't make mistakes. They are much more reliable than men.

MP: That's a matter of individual qualities. There's no question of being smarter, being more intelligent or being more likeable. (*Laughter*)

MD: No, I mean do *they* know that madness people talk about? Or is it exclusively human?

MP: Yes, they run. Besides they wear blinkers. But we can't put blinkers on.

MD: So you are all . . .

MP: We are all what?

MD: I don't know. How can I put it?

MP: We're horses?

MD: No. I spoke of horses because I like horses. I have a lot of respect for the creatures. A very great deal, in fact as much as for men. And horses don't have that. They don't suddenly become mad like that . . .

MP: How so? In a race they can start galloping. If it enters their head.

MD: Yes, they panic, it's true. It's true what you say. It's true.

MP: I find it hard enough to explain football, I certainly shan't manage to explain horse races! (*Laughter*)

MD: No, but the analogies are interesting.

MP: It's a fine world, the football world. You start from a passion at six years old and then you become somebody, thanks to football. For some people. Otherwise I would be a steelworker.

MD: It seems it was your father or your grandfather who noticed that you had a gift?

MP: No, football didn't exist in France. When I went to the town hall to ask for an official document, they read 'profession: footballer' and nobody believed it. That was fifteen years ago.

MD: Only fifteen years?

MP: Yes, football came into existence with the arrival of the Greens [St Etienne] in 1972-73. After that there was the French team. Before, it didn't exist. From 1958 to 1972 there was nothing. There was a bad spell because we don't have a sporting culture in France. So there will always be sterile periods. You take tennis, there's Noah, Leconte and then nothing. If Noah retires, there'll be just Leconte who ranks twelfth or even twenty-second at the moment. And then after that it's difficult. In motor racing there's Prost and after him we'll have a long wait. In cycling there was Hinault . . .

MD: Well, I was talking about tragic phenomena, tragic characters. Noah is a tragic character.

MP: Yes. I don't know about that. I don't much like talking about other people, judging them.

MD: Yannick's got everything, everything. He had looks as well. And the angelism I was talking about in connection with you. He had it too, completely. There were two of you in France.

MP: In an individual sport, you're on your own. In collective sports, you can hide behind a good team from time to time. He *must* win, and quite alone.

MD: Can you imagine that, to be alone facing your fate as a sportsman?

MP: Oh no! I was born in the world of football. Our life is built on friendship, we defend each other, we love each other. I could never have taken part in an individual sport.

MD: I often have the feeling, watching you, because

I've seen lots of your matches, that you were thinking more of the team than of yourself.

MP: Absolutely. Yes, of course. Ever since I became captain, that's to say in the eighties. In the French team I scored goals, so I knew the team needed me. And so I gave it everything. Whether it was a question of fame or of money, we always shared everything. It's a particular mentality. You can't go against your mentality.

MD: But it has to be said, too, that loneliness affects everybody as well. You know that.

MP: Yes. But at difficult moments, if I hadn't got on well with the team, they'd have dropped me. And at the end of the day they helped me too, to become what I am. They would have dropped me, no, for sure, you know, I can commit myself to the job in hand, the guy who has the ball, he's the one who's boss on the pitch. A fellow like Giresse, for example, if Giresse didn't like me, instead of setting me up for a goal, he could have said 'OK, that's it' and I wouldn't have scored all the goals I did. This can happen too, you know. It can happen.

MD: But the giving can't necessarily be seen. What is given is a state of mind. It's very profound. It's a need of each one and of them all, the need you have of them and the need they have of you. Without you, they are a group of individuals. When they know that you're with them, they're no longer a group of individuals, they attain a kind of ease, happiness, childhood. It's one person who *makes* the community, that's you, your role is to give them what they need.

MP: A need for confidence, a need for experience.

MD: Yes. It's magnificent. It's a kind of state, do you see, a faculty for stepping outside one's preferences and attaining a love for the community.

MP: There have been moments of grace.

MD: But even in despair. I remember the despair of the French team in Mexico. Argentina had won. Your despair was crushing. Amid the delirium, the chants, the yells of the crowd, I can still hear the silence of the French. Well, there you are . . .

MP: For us in Mexico, it was a question of moving France towards a game that was not just collective, because it was collective already, but much more extended, I mean football with a broader view. We were stronger than Germany. But we lost. We may not have been as good as Brazil. But we beat them. You go all over the world, you travel, everywhere in the world people are talking of French football. In a way we are the only thing French that people talk about, apart from scent, perhaps.

MD: And literature.

MP: And literature. Yes, but if you go among poor children in Indonesia or Malaysia, they won't be talking about French literature, unfortunately for them.

MD: I am translated in thirty countries. Thirty countries, that's more than Europe and America.

MP: Yes, but if you go into the favelas in Rio, I don't think literature is very important. On the other hand, football is very important indeed.

MD: Which regions are apprentice players to be found in?

MP: All over the place. Anywhere where there's room to play. In the East, in Lorraine there's plenty of room with the empty factories. Those are the recruiting grounds. Football is synonymous with poverty. The two countries where the least football is played are the two richest countries in the world: the United States and Japan.

MD: What makes the difference between a footballer of genius and one who is just very good?

MP: The trainers they've had, for sure.

MD: But you knew at fifteen.

MP: No, I didn't know anything. I knew at seventeen that I could be a professional. For thirty years I was in a closed environment. For the last six months I have been in a less closed environment, where I'm beginning to understand things more easily. It's normal. One can't do everything!

MD: Did you always dream of the footballer you would be?

MP: I always dreamed of football. Not of a footballer. I didn't know that one could be a footballer. For me, football, as I said, was playing in front of as many people as possible who enjoy watching. That was my aim.

MD: Yes, but it was you who was playing – I mean in your dream?

MP: Ah! It was me who was playing! Ah! It was me at the centre.

MD: So you see, for me, to be a footballer of genius like Michel Platini requires a vocation for martyrdom.

MP: Perhaps. I am going to tell you why I became a good footballer. It wasn't predictable. I hadn't the physical qualities to be a good footballer.

MD: About six foot . . . that's not short, you know.

MP: I was short when I was young. I mean, you know, when you join a junior team, there are the big boys who run fast and score goals, and then there are the small ones who, when they meet a defender, they can get past him once. The defender *recovers* because he's faster. Twice. So you learn to get past him, you learn to be smart, you learn to play against them . . .

MD: With your brains.

MP: That's right. Achilles against the tortoise. And you learn to be smarter, to play in terms of the qualities you've got. There are qualities that you've got. There are qualities that are basic. Until I was sixteen or seventeen, I would attempt to get past the defender six times before I got to the goal. But at eighteen, when I started to grow and to train, I did it once and I was at the goal; because he might be faster, the one who was fast, who was strong when he was small, who was good, who was king of the village, who ran faster than anyone else, but he was nothing any more, he didn't exist. So martyrdom for me was being small and perhaps that's what made me a good footballer. It's true.

MD: You weren't sorry to have grown, then. (*Laughter*)

MP: Well no, because once I had grown and I had caught up with the others, I made a difference, because I had other qualities.

MD: It was a complete experience?

MP: That's it, it was an experience. I had qualities of anticipation, being smart, seeing ahead, seeing clearly, making good passes. Because the ball, I was always told, my father told me, after all the ball goes faster than a man. So it was better to make the ball run fast than to run fast like it. And that's the basis of football. That's why I was criticised for not running, but you have to make the ball run, *we* don't have to run! I was criticised for not 'getting my shirt wet', that was the fashionable phrase. I was told 'You must tackle'; tackling, you know, is hurling yourself and taking the ball from an attacker's feet. Right. Well, I did that and I became a superplayer. But I kept my experience. I anticipate on the other man's qualities, his way of seeing things . . .

MD: Does it take intelligence to be a great footballer?

MP: Not necessarily. You have to be able to handle success, which is very difficult. I think it's difficult to be a great footballer for fifteen years. For one year it's easy.

MD: And during a game?

MP: During a match it's easy. There are players who've made their whole career on one match. You wouldn't know them, even if I told you their names. There are players who do everything to appear on television, who make a splash and then it's over. Afterwards, they play, but they live on their attainment. I've never lived on my attainment. Just as in life, I always know what lies ahead. The things that happen to me, I make happen. The move from football to my civilian life hasn't been difficult because I've a host of things to do.

MD: How old are you? What are you going to do?

MP: I'm thirty-two. I'm going to create a brand name and do advertising.

MD: On telly?

MP: Yes, on telly.

MD: You'd do it in Paris.

MP: Yes, on Canal Plus. And then I'll do some coproductions with RAI and Canal Plus. I am going to do reports on athletes, humorous, sympathetic reports to make people see that sport really is marvellous. Because when you talk about sport, or if you listen to sport nowadays, it's doping, it's violence, it's all rather negative. That's why I've always been at daggers drawn with the journalists. I don't like guys who judge others, who preach; I've been preached at all through my career, all my life I've been preached at. Well, I don't like it. I've been idolised, yes, but not by the journalists. Most of the journalists when I missed that penalty in Mexico, they were French, they stood up and were happy. Oh yes, I've got witnesses, I've got Italian journalists who've told me. Oh yes, I've been buggered about for fifteen years.

MD: How do you explain that?

MP: By the sort of person I am, because I've always been at loggerheads with them. I'm someone who tells them to bugger off, I don't want to answer them. I've been nasty and they've been nasty. OK. In the end we're on speaking terms again and we start afresh and remake our lives.

MD: Are you sure of what you said about Mexico?

MP: Oh yes! Italian journalists have confirmed it. Several of them. They've never given me names. Anyway, I know some of them. No, but that's my personal problem. If you've got personality, you can't please everyone. And to succeed, you have to have personality. When you train a team, you have to have personality so that they all follow you, a nice personality, not a nasty one.

MD: The extraordinary thing in your case is that there's nothing of a leader of men about you. You are shy.

MP: Yes, I'm very shy. But I've become a leader of men because people needed me. They trusted me, I gave them back their confidence. I've never been as good as when I've been pushed to the front. When I'm there in front and I accept responsibilities, then I'm good. If I hide behind somebody, I'm not good. So the day I started to stand up in front of people, I made an exceptional leap forward.

MD: You realised they were calling for you?

MP: Yes, they were calling for me. But afterwards, you need to be intelligent enough to accept it. We could have won the World Cup. But we only realised we were good, that we were one of the best teams in the world, when we lost to Germany in Seville. That was when we realised we were good. Starting from that moment, we won the European Championship and reached the semi-final in the World Cup and finished third. That was when we learnt we were good. When we were martyrs we learnt we were good.

MD: Is that a word you'd use, 'martyr'?

MP: Never, no. But you know, sportsmen will never make anyone weep over their fate with words like that, never.

MD: Is it very difficult to work through that? The unhappiness? The sadness? The despair?

MP: It's true, I show my feelings, I find it hard to hide them.

MD: But it's magnificent to live like that – no caution, no false modesty.

MP: Professionally it's a blemish.

MD: There's another like you in football, very tall with slightly curly hair. I believe it's Rocheteau.

MP: Ah, Dominique, that's true. He has the sad look of an angel. He's intelligent. It's true, we had a group of intelligent players. But Dominique – it's true that he had rather that angelism you talk of, but a martyred, sad angelism. He doesn't display his joy, Dominique, he never has shown joy. You occasionally saw him smile but only among ourselves, never on the pitch. Dominique will score, he'll be pleased, but he'll always be serious. Me, I'm Italian.

MD: That's shiningly obvious, you can't imagine.

MP: I can't manage to hide my feelings.

MD: And this business of identifying with the public. It was you who established it, it started with you. There are some others who can do it, but it started first and foremost with you.

MP: I never set out in public to try and understand people. I saw them in my own way, as I liked to see them, as people who go to football for pleasure. Up until May 1985. After that it gets complicated.

MD: What will your life revolve round now?

MP: Round my family.

MD: You've got two children?

MP: Yes, two, aged nine and seven. I should like to watch them grow up. I have seen them growing but I want to see them grow some more. And then after that I shall be involved with my brand name and with television.

MD: Your wife's not Italian?

MP: Originally, yes. Through her father. Her mother's Swiss.

MD: After which match was it that you went to find her in La Baule?

MP: After I'd been whistled at in the Parc des Princes. When the public told me to get out.

MD: It wasn't Heysel?

MP: No. No. It was when François Mitterrand became president. It was in 1981, against Stuttgart, a friendly with the French team and Mitterrand had just been elected a fortnight before. Afterwards I went back to play Paris St Germain. They whistled me again, but that was normal because I was with Juventus playing against Paris St Germain.

MD: Was that when he gave you the medal?

MP: No, that was in 1984.

MD: You remained on good terms with him?

MP: I'm on good terms with everybody. So long as nobody comes to pester me or tries to make use of me politically, I'm on good terms with everybody. (*Laughter*)

MD: I'm a friend of the President. I've interviewed him several times in a row. I laughed because I can't see François Mitterrand using you at all. What for? To do what?

MP: Politics is another world. As for me, the day there's a government that doesn't recruit its members from its party because they have the same ideas as it does, but recruits them from the people it deems to be best qualified to do the job, the best people, then I'll go along with it. Just as a French team exists that's selected from the best players in all the clubs, I think it's possible to form a government like that. The best are not necessarily your friends on the left or the right. For me, that's wrong from the start. Because I am conditioned. My life is football, and football conditions you.

MD: The football field, the place where the players play, where they are shut in, is a piece of theatre watched by the spectators, a place of confrontation, so it's already a political place. As soon as you've got something to play for, even just a simple win – one that's justified by insults – you're no longer playing just to play, you're playing against an enemy. And anything goes when it comes to tarnishing him, justifying his defeat. Nobody is innocent of that horror. Of course, there's no political equivalent for what happens in a stadium. But already there's rejection, racism – any word will do – *you've* never indulged in rejection, I'm sure.

MP: Never. That's true.

MD: There's a kind of pre-fascism, an innocent fascism that hangs around stadiums, just as it certainly does in schools, in universities, in members of political parties.

MP: You know, apart from a few examples where there are two sides in a stadium, at Parc des Princes, everyone's French or in London, they're all English.

MD: But I mean it's the same mood that underlies racism.

MP: I can't follow you into that area; it's one I don't know much about.

MD: Football has been a home for misogyny. A long while ago. Women didn't go to football.

MP: Politics too.

MD: Politics as well; that's over.

MP: It's over in football. There are female football teams all over the place.

MD: I was talking about women on the terraces. Women weren't taken to watch football because it was said they weren't capable of understanding it. Are you going to live in Paris?

MP: No. I live in Nancy.

MD: Do you have a plane?

MP: I do have a plane.

MD: That you pilot yourself?

MP: No.

MD: You've got a small plane?

MP: I've got a plane, a good plane, a jet.

MD: How long do you take from Nancy, half an hour?

MP: No, it's based at Marseille.

MD: And what do you use your plane for?

MP: I use it, for example, this evening, because tomorrow I've got to go to Zurich, and as I'm quite a busy man and because of planes that don't leave, I'm always losing two days in four, I take my own plane. Tomorrow I'm going to Zurich in my plane, I'm leaving at seven o'clock. It'll come and pick me up tomorrow morning and take me to Zurich, where I'm going to make the draw for the World Cup on satellite television.

MD: Why don't you do a sports newspaper?

MP: I do a column in *L'Equipe*. I do a piece on football every Sunday morning, too, on RTL. I'm becoming a journalist! I try to explain things calmly, to be uncontroversial, to explain . . . Football has one big disadvantage; it's that only one team can win. In everything. In the World Cup: one team. A championship: one team. And it's difficult. Because people take sides. It's bloody annoying.

MD: It's the same everywhere.

MP: It may be the same everywhere. In politics, too, there's only one winner. And in football the same. Everywhere.

MD: Does your wife work?

MP: She is working because she looks after the children. But she travels. I take her with me occasionally, we're taking the chance to travel while we're young. I took her to Toronto and I took her to Japan.

MD: Where did you meet her?

MP: In Nancy. She was doing economics.

MD: I went there not long ago . . . I did a piece on Christine Villemin.

MP: Ah yes, yes, yes. I've only been living there six months, in Nancy. I lived there for seven years earlier and I've been in Nancy six months now.

MD: It's a wonderful town.

MP: Ah, they've improved it a lot. That's Rossinot, the mayor.

MD: Have you bought a flat?

MP: No, a house. In the centre.

MD: Near the square?

MP: Yes, not far. Near the station. Have you been to Nancy by train?

MD: No, always by car. With a team from *Libé* [*Libération* the newspaper].

MP: Where were you staying? In a hotel?

MD: We were in Christine Villemin's village. In a good village hotel.

MP: That's in the Vosges.

MD: It's beautiful, very beautiful.

MP: The Vosges are all very well. In summer it's marvellous. In winter it's cold and there's snow. It's hard. Dreary. The people have no future there. What with the Vosges and the textiles . . .

MD: It's one of the unemployment black spots.

MP: In my region, the iron and steel industry is hell. The people are all out of work.

MD: I was told you didn't speak Italian as well as you do French.

MP: That depends; if I'm on the telly I speak Italian better than French. I've been spoilt by Italian television. Four years there. And they accepted errors in grammar, errors in the language, but in France, as I am French, it's difficult. So I'm very careful, and then, as I spoke Italian for five years, I go into a restaurant, for example, and I can say: can I *prenote* a table, which seems quite reasonable to me. So that's why I'm quite at home speaking Italian. And then, they love laughing, jokes, all that. In France I have to be very careful.

MD: Where in Italy do you come from?

MP: From Piedmont, near Turin. My grandparents.

MD: Lombardy?

MP: No, Piedmont, it's on the frontier.

MD: That's the flat, European Italy.

MP: That's right. The Po, the plain of the Po.

MD: It's gorgeous. There aren't many things in the world as beautiful. The whole valley. When I think of Italy now, I think of that. Even in Venice I think I prefer the Po Valley.

MP: It's quieter. There aren't so many tourists.

MD: That's right, that's right. There's something restful about it. I think it's the Po itself. It reminds me of the rivers in Indo-China: it's massive and slow.

MP: But it can turn angry quickly.

MD: Yes, it rises fast. That region – I've never seen it all – the end of the Po, the great hunting region?

MP: On the Adriatic?

MD: Not directly.

MP: There's the Veneto, near Verona.

MD: No. It's beyond Verona. There are a lot of estates. It's not far from Comacchio, the Venice of the eel fishers.

MP: I've never played in Comacchio, so I can't say. Our life is made up of hotels, stadiums, it's difficult to go for a walk, you don't have time. Our life as footballers, what was it? Training, resting, playing; training, resting, playing. Nothing else.

©*Libération*, 1987.

(Conversation published on 14 and 15 December 1987)

Translated by Mary Turton.

once upon a time . . .

RITA LEE

Sir Football was a renowned Englishman who travelled abroad in order to colonise natives and force them into field labour. He landed in Brazil where to his delight he found indigenous people, bananas and voodoos.

'This is going to be a piece of cake,' he thought through his top-hat.

And he didn't waste any time. With his fierce hooligan soldiers he initiated his evil doings by challenging a local tribe that was observing their antics with suspicion and mockery. 'Pretty nice Jesuits, don't play too bad, call the chief to have a look.'

The noble Englishman gesticulated, shouted, commanded, while also trying to hide tactical aspects of the game. Chief Pelé enters the field. He takes hold of the ball, smells it, shakes the foreign 'coconut' and starts showing exotic tricks (later to be known as 'embaixadas') which the Englishmen imagined to be some sort of homage paid by the chief to show submission. In reality, it was a sign for the natives to assume their positions on the pitch for an all-out attack. Sir Football and his hooligans came close, I mean really close, to being transformed into bowling pins, which would have consequently changed the name of the game forever.

Chief Pelé and his tribe didn't give the Englishmen a

chance to get near, let alone touch the ball (this is the origin of the current Brazilian expression 'for English eyes only').

But they finally managed to have a penalty called in their favour, the score already being more than 1,000 goals to 0 for the natives. The situation was chaotic, when suddenly Sir Football had the brilliant idea to offer a bet. 'Your kingdom for a goal!!!'

Chief Pelé accepted, and to everyone's astonishment, went to lie down in his hammock for a nap. Sir Football himself got into position to take the penalty, made ready, smirked a malicious smile, and kicked . . . kicked hard . . . kicked with class . . . and hit the post! It was a nice post made up of two charming banana trees that, with the ball's impact, dropped a bunch of bananas into the goal, adding the final touch to the Englishmen's humiliation.

Contrary to legend, Sir Football didn't end up the main course at the natives' victory banquet. He did, though, humbly substitute his top-hat (as now a symbol of power) for a coloured gourd, and departed with a few remaining odds and ends, for England. It is said that he changed his name to 'Futebol' to be able to enter his Kingdom unnoticed.

As for the hooligans, they never managed to play again and so formed a sort of guerrilla brotherhood known to operate undercover among English football fans.

Pelé is well known today all over the world as the biggest 'Top-Hat' hunter around. His collection is visited daily by people from all over the world who are interested in the art of scoring more than 1,000 goals per game.

di' france ting

EMMA LINDSEY

I - Coming home

This whole football thing leaves me cold. In fact the first time I went to a live football match was with the *Observer*'s then chief football correspondent, Patrick Barclay, in 1995. We went to watch West Ham play. Not a thrilling match but with it my football cherry was plucked although I was still none the wiser. My white colleagues were shocked that I had never before known the ecstasy of sitting in the cold watching a ball being kicked from one end of a pitch to the other. But then I ask, how many black women have you ever seen at a football match? Like I said, this whole football thing leaves me cold – or did until Jamaica looked like they were in with a chance of qualifying for the World Cup.

There's a reason for that. Historically, the main point of football in Britain has been to give white, working class men a structure to their leisure time, an opportunity to bond in a primal way. It also gave women a chance to do the housework unhindered or have a natter with their mates. Ethnic minorities of either sex didn't really figure. Today the game has a social currency which it has never had before. But the presence of black people off the pitch is so faint as to be nearly invisible. The legacy of hooliganism and racial violence is part of the reason, the other part is more complex.

Ask most black people in Britain who they support in the World Cup and Brazil, Cameroon and Nigeria will be on the list. It's not about nationality, it's about seeing your own. Jamaica's qualification for the World Cup was the first time football came straight home and no messing, to us. It came home to those among the 2.3 million black people living here with Jamaican roots (and to those without), as well as to Jamaicans in America, Canada and elsewhere, and to black men, women and children across the diaspora. For the *Windrush* pioneers, now senior citizens, the team's initial success was a landmark in post-colonial evolution.

Who said it was just a game?

II – Nuhbaddy trouble you dis side

Indirectly it was sport which took me to Jamaica for the first time and I didn't like the place much. I went in July 1996, during the Atlanta Olympics, when sprinter Michael Johnson boasted his talent in golden spikes. I was one black woman in a party of white men, on a sports freebie, passed my way by a generous sports editor. Ostensibly we were checking out the sports facilities at an all-inclusive near Montego Bay, this was to be a total tourist experience, club class all the way. I sat next to a radio journalist on the plane who, after establishing that I wasn't Jamaican, asked me if I would be able to translate patois for him.

On my first morning, I was up at five. Too excited to go back to sleep, I threw back the curtains to see that it was raining. I went for a walk anyway, the rain was warm. Running down into the sea was a ring-chain fence, next to it a small wooden hut, empty. I was making my way around the fence when a low voice startled me: 'A'fe leave your room number.'

I turned to find the voice belonged to a security guard who definitely wasn't in the hut when I arrived.

'Na mon. You can't go past here, it dangerous that side. You might not make it back.'

A woman who had walked up to the fence called out, 'Don't listen to 'im. Nuhbaddy trouble you dis side, nuh budda wid dat. 'Im try and sceer ya. Com.'

The woman kissed her teeth. There was an angry exchange between her and the guard. By this time a few people had gathered on the other side of the fence, all of them urging me to 'com'. So I walked past him, now glowering in his box. It turned out the other side was a public beach, not bought by our hotel. It was scrubby, pebbly, a left-over, discarded for use by the local people. Nothing did trouble me, except what a typical white, British tourist, on a first trip to a black country with nothing but stories of Yardies to light the way, might have made of the situation.

The all-inclusive lived up to its claim. Everything was included in the £1,100 per week price. Everything was on site, even gift shops and a post office. Unless you wanted to go on a tour organised by the hotel, there was no reason to leave. I came to think of it as a compound.

Most package tourists never actually touch down in Jamaica. There is as a result a total lack of understanding or respect on both sides of the tourist fence. I once overheard a woman at my gym describing her holiday in Barbados. The highlight seemed to be having rum punch

In the hotel with nowhere to go.

brought out to her on a li-lo in the sea, by hotel staff in a rowing boat. Another instance. I was telling a colleague about P. J. Patterson, the Jamaican prime minister, when she interrupted: 'Does Jamaica have a prime minister then?' shocked.

Most folk, if they stop to think about the island at all, think of it as a jumble of images peppered with characters: Bob Marley, limbo dancers, Yardies, ganja-smoking rastas, Lilt adverts and cricket players. There is no sense of it as a country, as distinct from the rest of the Caribbean as England is from France.

III – Jamaica get your passports
16 November 1997, London

There's a huge queue snaking down the steps outside the York Hall in Bethnal Green. Everyone here has abandoned a Sunday night in to watch Jamaica play their final

World Cup qualifying game against Mexico via a satellite link. Over 3,000 people squeeze into the historic boxing venue. The atmosphere is unlike anything at a typical sporting event in Britain; for a start, the only white faces belong to camera crews and the odd journalist. For the first time ever, in a hall full of strangers I don't feel on my own.

This is a poke in the eye of everyone who thought black people don't watch football. We do, it's just that most black fans prefer to stay at home or go to each other's houses to watch matches on cable TV. British football culture, with pubs forming a large part, is fairly alien to the ways in which black people like to enjoy themselves.

It's a family vibe. Kick off is at 7 p.m., ten minutes to go. Most people have already sat down on the wooden school chairs arranged in rows in front of the screen at the end of the hall, the rest stand. Soon there is a fuzzy picture of the National Stadium in Kingston. A cheer crashes around the hall, horns blare although nothing has happened yet. A draw would be sufficient for Jamaica to get through. Then snowy interference takes over and the screen goes black. Winston Clarke, the sports promoter whose idea this was, takes it in his stride and the game resumes to everyone's relief. By half-time a draw is looking likely, and people are standing on their chairs.

In the second half, saves and mad goalmouth scrambles combined with Mexico defending without much conviction – they're off to France in any case – ratchets the tension. Then after a blizzard renders the players a pointillist abstraction, the picture snaps out. The public are less obliging this time and Clarke offers refunds.

Miraculously whatever has befallen the satellite receiver is rectified and we watch, as the minutes tick past and Mexico fail to make an impression. Just before the final whistle, everyone is leaping up and down, tears are streaming, horns are blaring. 'Jamaica get your passports,' shouts the DJ and cranks up the music.

IV - Ballers from foreign

Picture the scene: Portsmouth farting about at the arse end of the First Division, fighting relegation, and Paul Hall and Fitzroy Simpson, wingers with a tight double-act, decide they want to try to get to the World Cup with Jamaica.

Paul Hall at twenty-six has more personality than many could ever dream of. He DJs on the side. A dinky striker with an upturned nose and a cheeky expression, who seems on the permanent verge of laughter, he says: 'Portsmouth knew we wanted to play for Jamaica. They told us they'd sent a fax to the Jamaican Football Federation (JFF) to say that we were available and that we'd been selected for the Jamaican team.'

But then a friend in the team let on it was a trick. Paul called the JFF and discovered the alleged fax had never been sent.

'I felt really upset, man. I'd told everyone I'd been selected, my mum, my aunties, everyone. I said to Fitzy, "We've got to do this ourselves."' So the two of them, along with Deon Burton, a former team-mate who'd gone to Derby County, spent their own money on flights and accommodation and went to Jamaica for trials.

They made the team. 'So the joke backfired on them, really,' Hall says charitably.

Football can get very ugly.

Now Paul feels honoured to play for the country of his parents' birth. When he tries to describe his feelings, his appreciation for the welcome Reggae Boyz fans have given the team, he gets lost for words, because he's never felt anything like it before.

Back home in England they couldn't quite get their heads round it. Although for Portsmouth, football exchange between England and Jamaica was a case of history repeating itself. In 1947 the first Jamaican to earn a regular place on a First Division team was signed to Portsmouth: 'Lindy' Delapenha. Rave reviews were heaped on him. In 1950 he went to Middlesbrough. When Brian Clough, Lindy's team-mate, was asked why he never took penalties, he replied: '. . . because Lindy never bloody misses.'

The 'ballers from foreign' got their chance with Jamaica after a punch-up in Mexico City. In April 1997, a friendly fixture was set up between the Reggae Boyz and a local side, Toros Neza. It was intended to be a practice match, since the team had suffered a humiliating 6-0 defeat against Bolivia the previous month and almost died in the process – unaccustomed as they were to thin air. Well, that was the plan. What happened was a massive brawl. An Argentinian playing for the Mexicans attacked a Jamaican, which was enough to clear the bench, as they say in basketball circles. Punches, dropkicks, sticks and bricks flew. Onandi Lowe got a broken wrist, and even Rene Simoes, Jamaica's Brazilian coach, was socked in the jaw.

Although video footage showed the Reggae Boyz didn't start it, smacked bottoms from FIFA were dispensed in the form of fines for the Mexican football federation, and both teams.

Next Jamaica lost 6-0 to Mexico in a World Cup qualifier.

By this point the team had made it through three Caribbean qualifying zones. Although some, like Peter 'Miles on the clock' Cargill, the team's oldest member, had a suitable approach to their job, others had a problem, like packing up and going home in the middle of a tournament if the mood took them, or missing training. It didn't take long for Simoes to sort it. He dished out fines and sermonising tellings-off. Disciplinarian yes, over the top – maybe sometimes – but it seemed to work. They conceded only six goals in his first eight matches, but still they needed back-up.

Simoes started punching the overseas digits in June 1997 and by September the English influx had begun. Hall, Simpson, Burton and Robbie Earle – although he was scarce until later on – were the first professional 'ballers from Hinglan' to join up.

When they first went over to 'Jamdown' it was no picnic, except for Earle. He was spared having to sleep on the team camp floor. Instead a presidential suite in a five-star hotel and limo awaited him in Kingston.

And the girls. Although footballing hysteria was a brand new thing in Jamaica, the groupies could have taught their English cousins a lot about technique. There was a queue of women waiting for one or all of the Reggae Boyz to etch themselves on their hearts. Or at least autograph the bosom of their tee shirts. With one phone in the team house filled with twenty-two men, it was easy to see why the mobile became such a vital piece of equipment. In Jamaica having an assortment of women to call on is the norm. Paul was quite shocked and a teeny bit scared by Jamaican women's full-on approach.

It wasn't the only difference between the two countries. In Jamaica there is not the same sense of urgency, to say the least. Earle's wife commented how difficult it was to establish from the JFF simple details like a list of hotels where the team would be staying.

No one actually came right out and said it, but there was an undercurrent in English football clubs that their Jamaicans were being ungrateful. The Division One volunteers going, people could sort of understand, but Wimbledon's Earle and Marcus Gayle and later Chelsea's Frank Sinclair? They were just looking for a bit of fun in the sun and shirking their domestic duties.

It was all right for Jack Charlton to do it for Ireland, Craig Brown to do it for Scotland, but it was not all right for some bloke from Brazil to come here and take 'our players' to play for some marijuana-smoking football outfit in Jamaica! Of all places. They could not be serious.

Oh but they were. Playing for Jamaica was no joking matter. In the 100 or so years that black players have been seen in professional English football – Arthur Wharton was the first (pity him) back in 1898 – they have come a long way.

V - Big up
January 1998, Jamaica
The breeze wafts a heat of many layers. Within five minutes of stepping off the plane, I'm too hot in jeans and a tee shirt.

I'm here because I am compelled to find out where the

Reggae Boyz have sprung from – these boys who are in fact grown men. Jamaica is the star of the Caribbean thanks to qualifying for the World Cup. In Britain some people wonder what the shoeless inhabitants of a tourist destination could possibly know about the technical difficulties of football, they speculate whether the players will all sport dreadlocks, wandering around the pitch lost in a fug of ganja smoke. People feel quite affectionate towards the 'plucky West Indians'. Of course they don't stand a chance but certainly promise to be a colourful addition to the tournament. A sort of 'mascot team', if you will.

In Jamaica, everyone – from the most senior of citizens to the youngest basketball-playing kid – breaks into proud smiles about the national football team. It is as if someone in the family has suddenly made it as a mega-bucks film star. Generally people feel this 'france ting' is a chance to stamp Jamaica's authority on the rest of the world. And when Jamaica bring home that cup, it will be Jah scoring for the island.

Kingston is really hot. Outside, away from the protection of air conditioning, just walking down the street is an experience in overheating. The combination of no breeze, few trees and lots of concrete means the sun bakes the heat into the streets. When cars zoom past, dust from the road flies up and sticks to the fine sweat on your skin. Downtown, jackets of suits spend most of the time draped over office chairs and are rarely worn.

Jamaica Life, the island's biggest insurance company, has cool offices. Behind smoked glass, its employees have helped finance the team's trip to France with an in-house sales competition, 'Fly the Gate in '98'. In return the JFF have donated a few prized World Cup tickets.

Inside Captain Horace Burrell and Simoes, guests of honour, are propelled amid a bustle of the suited into the conference suite. One tall, the other short, one a black Jamaican, the other a white Brazilian, both with substantial moustaches. Simoes, with his Mr Potato Head nose, big glasses and opulent facial hair, looks like he's in disguise. Burrell, straight man to the Brazilian, just looks pleased.

The breadman, as Burrell is sometimes called, kicks off the morning's speechifying, bass tones booming through the mike, pausing every so often for effect, his cheeks bunched up with smiles.

'Of all walks of life how can little Jamaica make it to the World Cup?' he asks rhetorically. 'Big question. We did . . .' He obviously likes public speaking. 'How can little Jamaica make it through the first qualifying round in France?' A pause, 'We will.'

When the thunderous clapping subsides, he says: 'Now, without any further ado, I shall turn you over to my sparring partner.'

Simoes bounds up to the lectern: 'As you know my natural language is Portuguese so every time I have to face the auditorium I get a little *nirvous*, but I try.' Fond laughter from the audience who, like the rest of Jamaica, see him as a saviour. He tells a story which he's obviously told many times before: 'I was instructor teaching coaches from around the world at the Brazilian football academy when the president invited me to come to Jamaic'. I listened, hey he's a big guy but I said no, is a beautiful cunt' but I don't want go Jamaic'. I came here in 1989 with Brazilian Under-20 national team and then I think Jamaic' is below zero, nothing football.'

What he lacks in height he makes up for in charisma, this ebullient South American with a salesman's patter and innate sense of timing. He waits for the laughter to die down, then tells the story about when he and Burrell first met.

'When the Captain saw a short guy in jeans and tee shirt, he thought I was a driver,' says Simoes.

Knowing Burrell, proud of his Sandhurst training, you can just imagine it.

'He wanted me to take him to the Copacabana Plaza Hotel. Well in the sixties it was four star hotel, in the seventies, two star, and now it has closed down.'

'I called the Foreign Affairs minister and I said "Listen, I think this guy is mad, he calls the Brazil government, asks to come here, thinks the government is going to pay his hotel bill and that I am his driver." ' It is impossible not to warm to the man.

It has been said, albeit on the quiet, that being a white Brazilian with what is euphemistically called 'universal appeal' has helped enormously in developing the public relations paraphernalia at home. In Jamaica, much as anywhere else, lightness of complexion is valued. In banks, hotels, insurance companies, most senior positions belong to those of a fairer hue.

Simoes preaches: 'You have to identify your talent then you have to dream. That's the secret of the Reggae Boyz. We dream, we try, we fail but then you complain, get frustrated and don't do anything more. But we have to try again.'

No one actually says 'Amen' but it wouldn't be inappropriate; the Jamaica Life crowd are rapt in sentiment. Applause wells up from the auditorium, as the folk who make a living selling what nobody wants to buy – life insurance – rise to their feet. Simoes gestures for them to sit down.

'I am not better than God,' he proclaims leaning forward, his hands outstretched on the lectern, moustache quivering. Behind his Calvin Klein glasses, his eyebrows shoot up steeple-like. The audience is silent, perhaps stunned by the statement perhaps not. Jamaicans love the references to religion. His parables and biblical boomerangs go down a treat. Most of the time Simoes walks around in a 'Jesus Saves' tee shirt – he must have several – but for this occasion he wears a neat black suit.

Later that day everyone, including some goats, is waiting for the team's training session at the National Stadium.

Finally the team bus turns up. White and green with a yellow stripe, it has 'The Road to France 98' painted on the side and back. The players tumble out, shorts hanging lopsided, shirts out, some wearing trainers, others in flip-flops, but all dripping with gold jewellery.

Aaron Lawrence is a tall, gentle guy. Nicknamed 'Wild Boy' because he isn't, he is building a house with the money he's getting from football.

Peter Cargill's brow is permanently furrowed. He says he's thirty-four, others put him closer to forty. Whatever; he played professionally in Israel for eight years, and for a while John Barnes was his team-mate. They are still friends. Now he plays for a club called Harbour View with Ricardo Gardner. He looks stern, since he rarely smiles. But he's not unpleasant, just serious. Because he's been around, seen that whatever happens night follows

The whole island was ready for Jamaica's World Cup experience.

day, he's sceptical about the celebrity the team has acquired.

Walter Boyd is a sweet-voiced 'yout' with wonky teeth and an acne-scarred face. He hardly seems the monster he is made out to be. Known also as 'Blacka Pearl', he is later to be christened the Jamaican Gazza for his reputation for being brilliant but stroppy. Paul Hall says he is 'a real Yard Man', and very talented. But if Simoes says left, Boyd says right – for the hell of it. Like some of the other players, Boyd comes from an impoverished background. Poor but dignified.

Like Ian 'Pepe' Goodison, a hard-headed defender with a sharp football mind. He comes from an area called Olympic Gardens. Back then it was a war zone, now it's just down at heel. It's not somewhere a foreigner should venture alone; questions would be asked, there would be hassle but it's highly unlikely – despite the stories you hear – that you'd get shot. Nevertheless life in those concrete complexes, in the deodorant-defying heat, quite apart from the inconvenience of poverty, can't be pleasant. There are constant disagreements among the gangs who 'run tings' in the different neighbourhoods. The police don't seem too bothered; burglaries can happen right under their noses without them being too concerned. In some empty, dusty streets are the burnt-out shells of cars left in the road to block unwanted visitors from entering. Along the main road into downtown Kingston are the wrecks of buildings burnt down for some reason. A For Sale sign – selling what, you wonder – is stuck onto a rusted pole.

Yet it is from this environment that Pepe and some of the other players come. Although outside may look like Beirut on a bad day, inside their homes are pristine. The latest sound systems play the latest dancehall and American imports. Top-notch televisions show satellite channels while a nice car will sit outside.

They call Pepe 'The Terminator', he plays like that too, with his lower jaw stuck out in a permanent sulk.

Dean Sewell is as polished as Pepe is rough. A right-back with Constant Spring, he left his studies at an American university to join the Reggae Boyz' cause.

The ballers are bigger celebrities now than music's meteor-stars, Beenie Man, Bounti Killa and Red Rat put together. But the egos of the dancehall DJs aren't competing. Everyone accepts that football comes first. Besides there is a tradition of music and football hitting it off. Bob Marley was a near-obsessive footballer.

Dark grey clouds roll back like a curtain over the blue mountains, to present the late afternoon sun. Rays pick out the pink, yellow and blue seats in the stand like tropical flowers, and the different hues of brown on the green pitch, as the team do some warm-ups. So does reggae veteran Jimmy Cliff, bending, stretching and doing sprightly knee raises on old, stick legs. Sharp in new Nike trainers, and baseball cap, he looks like a walking advert.

Slow-talking sweeper Onandi Lowe, the tallest man in the team, pulls off his jacket and looks like an iron-clad god. I've never seen an all-black team of professional footballers play, except on telly; I had wondered what if any differences there will be. The most striking thing is the colours. The bright green of their shorts and dazzling yellow of their tops look triumphant. A lot of gold too. Chunky chains, each link a solid weight in your hand, rings like knuckledusters, all with individual designs. And their hairstyles. A lot of effort must go into keeping those plaits, cornrows, twists up to scratch. But here in Jamaica no one would expect anything less.

At one end of the stadium, in place of a scoreboard, is the Jamaica flag, underneath are words from the national anthem: Jamaica Land We Love.

The next evening, an hour before kick-off against Sweden, car stereos blast bashment sounds, the whistles have started already, notching up the heat of the night. Women dressed up for the occasion, looking fine, men scrubbed up, just looking. The stadium is pretty full, but not packed because it's only a friendly against Sweden. In the bleachers, guarded behind a high-wire fence, are those who can't afford seats. They are quiet. Concentrated. These tickets cost a lot of money, they're here to watch the match, give critical appraisal. The music is loud, the dancing showing off.

At the end of the night it's a 0-0 draw which is disappointing but not tragic. Outside the stadium a guy called Howard Chamber leans against the barrier. He came up with the design that was painted on the team bus for a competition. No one paid them for the design. 'We ave fe pay $4,000 fe bill it,' he says. He does it for the dream. 'If you look in the bible it say a small island gonna run the worl', and I tink it Jamaica.'

VI - Last call fi' get 'pon de bus
London to Kingston flight 002, May 1998
Surprisingly the Boyz sit bunched up in the economy section of the Air Jamaica flight from London, so I'm surrounded. Long legs jammed up against seat backs, scrunched-up tracksuit tops folded into awkward pillows serve those who want a kip. A stockpile of jet lag has left its mark. Paul Hall has buried his head in the seat-back in front of him.

Simoes had planned a twenty-seven-match warm-up schedule and by golly he has stuck to it. His rationale is that the team can learn in six months what would otherwise take five years. That they can pack it all in, in some kind of football roadshow.

Being stuck with the same group of people for months can't be much fun. Fitzroy Simpson, who along with Hall and 'Neon' Deon was one of the early pioneers, paying their own way and all that, was pissed off that others, who'd seemingly made less effort, had more of the limelight. Earle was the first to make the news big time about joining up for Jamaica. Smart, articulate and possessing a winning way with the media, Earle wrote a regular column for the *Observer*, then got picked to write another for the *Evening Standard* during the World Cup. Fitzy joked – but many a true word – about refusing to say anything unless I paid him. Why didn't someone want to write a book about him, he wondered when he heard that Earle had been asked to write his memoirs.

'His experiences? Ha. What the hell could he write about? He's never bloody here. What could he say about the Jamaican players? He never spends any time with them.' I explained that someone else would be writing the book. 'Good job,' he snorted, very pissed off.

Not on the plane is Walter Boyd. Blacka had gone too far in February when he failed to make a mandatory appearance at the Sports Personality of the Year award. Whether there was a link with the fact that it was his team-mate 'Neon' Deon Burton who won the accolade, is another matter.

Blacka had made his name as a forward from Nanny-ville. One thousand residents blocked traffic to protest that their man should be reinstated in the team. When this seemed to have no effect, death threats – serious, not idle – were launched the technical director's way. Many felt the Brazilian simply wanted to assert his power over Boyd. But Simoes had ignored the bullet-proof vest issued for his protection by JFF staff. The saga has done for his popularity in many quarters.

Beenie Man is on the plane with us, in a red straw beenie hat tied with a cream silk band. He is an ardent fan of the team and keeps bursting into song. For some people all the world's a stage, even the 002 to Kingston. You can't help staring at his gold watch with chunks of diamonds the size of peanuts on the strap, on his other wrist a diamond-studded gold-link bracelet, on his finger a conglomeration of diamonds. On the cuff of his houndstooth checked jacket the Moda Italia tag has been left on. In between flamboyant pit stops to the back of the plane for mammoth shots of brandy, and when that runs out he raids his own stock of Hennessy. It becomes a mini-concert with the JFF bigwigs, stretched out in First Class, coming back to enjoy it.

Finally after ten hours and a vigorous session of 'Captain Bird In Your Seat Aerobics' with the flight attendants, we touch down in JA. Everyone claps and we file off the plane into the moist warmth of the night. Since I've been sitting in the midst of the players, I experience along with them the welcome of flashing lightbulbs, television cameras and, of course, the Japanese.

That's where the share of preferential treatment ends. As I wait for what seems like an hour for my bags, they saunter through customs and onto their team bus which careers off into the night accompanied by police escort sirens. Not as you might think to the crisp cool sheets of a luxury hotel bed. Oh no. They are headed, whether they like it or not, to an all-night concert called 'Rise Up' staged in their honour. Conk Out might have been more apt.

A word or two on the Japanese. A television crew has been stationed in Jamaica for months, recording every move of the Reggae Boyz entourage. In that time their dress sense has evolved into weird rasta-hat-wearing and the donning of Bob Marley tee shirts. All this despite an interesting knack of avoiding any interaction with Jamaicans.

Kingston

The team are out on yet another public engagement, all is quiet. The players' den is an ordinary bungalow set in a large garden. A hibiscus bush reigns rampant. Through the bars on the windows – in Jamaica every good home has them – you can see a family-sized kitchen taken up by a big dining table and chairs stacked high with metal trays of bananas and watermelon. On the wall a map of Brazil. Next to the kitchen, mattresses on the floor neatly lined up with peachy sheets and in the background the blare of a massive television. At the back of the house the utility room is stuffed with free weights and exercise bikes. Two bare-chested men are sorting the washing and it is then the spy is espied and a bloke appears, shouting; then a woman from the kitchen with a large knife. It isn't aimed at me but it is disconcerting.

Just in time, back from tarting about, the team arrive and Hall and Simpson take charge and show me their bedroom. Spared the hardship of roughing it on the floor, Paul and Fitzy share bunk beds while Burton's divan lies in state in what has been dubbed the foreign players' room.

By British standards it is all a bit basic. There are no frills. And that in the long run has probably helped bring them all closer together.

Like the ingredients in a big pot of stew, the players have come together and got along, more or less. The English boys, instead of munching baked beans on toast, get good home-cooking: yam, dumpling, rice and pasta along with the usual meat, fish or ox-tail. Those Jamaican-born players who'd never been anywhere else, get a taste of what it might be like to play abroad.

Denise Nichols, team physio and 'mother to some, big sister to some, bredren to some', is the only woman to be with the guys around the clock. She says: 'They all enjoy the same music, they all wear the same kind of clothes even though there are different levels of education. There's all kinds of schooling going on at different levels.'

The foreign 'Bredren' have by and large been taken to the Jamaicans' hearts. Burton has even been honoured with the nickname 'Neon' Deon, the bright light in the side. At Derby County he had been spending a fair amount of time on the bench, before finding his calling in the Caribbean. Aside from becoming the island's heart-throb, with pages of the gossip tabloid *Xtra* given over to his supposed sexploits, the monosyllabic one has scored four goals in as many World Cup qualifying matches.

The gala do at the Prime Minister's house in Vale Royal, with dinner plates priced at £100 a head, promises to be a top-of-the-range night.

As you walk through the gates to the sweet lilting of fiddlers playing folk music, the first sight is a wedding cake of a bush, garlanded by tiny red and white fairy lights. More of them are draped around the islands of bushes, and along the awning of the Great House. Silver service waitresses tiptoe on the springy night grass with trays of iced wine. On a stage with coloured lights, Byron Lee and the Dragonaires are warming up.

And then out of the scented darkness comes an abbreviated 'weeoow' of a police siren. The guests of honour have arrived.

Dressed in smart black suits – thankfully not the houndstooth they'd worn before – with the team logo on the breast pockets, they file in, as handsome as soldiers on military parade. They've spent the day at a small water-falls and spa tucked away in the hills, and it shows. Rested for once and bright eyed, they look ready for a dressed-up evening out.

Everyone is called to take their places at white-linen covered tables under the stars. The Prime Minister isn't there, he's often away, it doesn't matter, instead 'King' Pelé holds court. And the speechifying begins. Simoes speaks, of course. His pretty daughter speaks – she's looking for a career in television, something tells me she'll find it – and Burrell speaks, a bit like a World Service news announcer. Then Pelé gets up and everyone rises. He talks about the 'special of the moments for football in Jamaica' and jokes about the possibility of his country and theirs meeting in the World Cup final. 'No doubt,' he says charmingly, 'you are the top in the world today.' Everyone claps, apart from a few of the Japanese who have nodded off.

The Jamaican Reggae Boyz sit with their girlies at the top table while Paul and Fitzy, the only English present – again – are shared out between two tables of important guests. Next to me is a group of white Jamaicans, speaking in startlingly broad accents, about how they'd been abroad to follow the team. Once the show had got on the road they had joined in the football mania. It is odd to see the same debate ongoing as in England as to who is or isn't a 'true' supporter.

Paul enjoying the evening, starts to talk about his mother. She would have been proud to see her son here.

'My dad left when I was four. I've only started to get to know him recently.'

You can tell it's given him a highly developed sense of responsibility. Although he's always ready with a joke, and he's a masterful mimic, he's also careful, discreet. Never has a bad word to say about anybody.

'I would never turn my back on any of my kids, you're going to need them one day. My mum gets everything now. She gets television people coming to her house, newspaper people, everybody in Birmingham is biggin' her up. It must be punishing for him now. Even if you and the mother can't get on, you should make the time to see your kids.'

A woman on the next table is quite drunk. She stretches as far across the table toward Fitzy as is decent and croons. He gives us a sideways wink.

Summoned by Burrell to take the platform the Reggae Boyz slowly walk up, Ricardo 'Bibi' Gardner slouching, hands in his pockets, his head cocked to one side. Next to him his mate Pepe Goodison, that jaw stuck out, in a copycat stance. Peter Cargill looks like their older brother. Theodore Whitmore, with his wild, bushman hair, punctuates the incongruous line-up. There they stand, in a straggly row, slightly embarrassed, Jamaica's footballing hopes.

Looking surly because it wouldn't be cool to smile, the motley crew say something about faith, hope and a fresh start. They have come a long way. But they still have far, far to go.

Then midnight strikes and the night's last dance is bounced out to Byron Lee and his Dragonaires. The monied have had a few drinks, chatted with friends and rediscovered a little romance. The women with aching feet carry their kitten heels in one hand, their partners by the other. Everyone is feeling good on the island's victory vibe.

The next evening, by the pool at the Wyndham hotel, Aaron Lawrence's mother smiles with pride for her son. The following day is Mother's Day and the hotel has arranged a lunchtime function, the JFF is paying. The sun has cooled down, but it is still up. Frankie Beverley sang about the 'golden time of day' with the soul group Maze; he must have written it in Jamaica. The blue pool is dappled with the light, and at 7.00 it is just the right time to indulge in a shot of dark rum, slice of fresh lime and chilled coke. The team, these days booked into the Wyndham, have finished training and are lounging in flip flops and shorts.

'I'm so proud of 'im,' says Mrs Lawrence, her high-pitched voice rising at the end, and she nods in agreement with herself.

'People come up to you, when you say you are a Reggae Boyz mother, everyone want to know you. And I bring 'im up on my own. Mmhmm. Now the father has come back, 'im want fe my boy to buy 'im a ky-ar.'

She tosses her head, then pats her hair, pursing her lips.

In Jamaica it's no biggie for a woman to bring up a whole family on her own.

I ask her if any of this, the celebrity, the money – paltry by English football standards – has changed him.

She says: 'No.' Thinks a bit, then says: ''Im get tired more, sleep more.' I'll bet.

Denise Nichols arrives in a dress and a touch of make-up instead of a track suit for once. 'I thought my boys looked so smart last night,' she says. 'Other countries must think Jamaica coming to the World Cup is like the country boys coming in. Our guys are so dead cool, though, they will style it out.'

So cool, at times they are frozen and I complain that although they stay at the same hotel and bump into me frequently, the majority still will not be lured into conversation beyond 'good morning'. I tell her stories about the goings-on at the top level of football. She tuts at Paul Gascoigne's drinking habits and when I tell her about the team's mid-air japes after playing in Hong Kong before Euro 96, her eyes are wide open. Her boys – she can't even imagine a similar scene. It's easy to see why the team call her 'Mommy'.

VII – Di' france ting

In the humid, grey afternoon before their deflowering, the team sit in stupor, isolated at their French hotel. Bored out of their minds, tired and seething with resentment, they wait for the World Cup. The guys watch the other teams jump from the aeroplane ahead of them.

Paul, sharing his room with Steve 'Shorty' Malcolm, confesses on his mobile phone (Simoes has taken away the room telephones) to feeling 'a bit like when the teacher is collecting in homework and everyone else has done it but you know you haven't'.

'I was watching South Africa play France last night,' he says, 'and it hit home for the first time that we're in the competition. It didn't feel too good because they're in the same situation as us and they didn't play too well. You can't help but draw comparisons.'

Watching Spain getting a collective ass-whipping by

Nigeria's Super Eagles was thrilling but unhelpful. Despite this, Paul says: 'We've got to take our chance, just go and treat it like any other game.' Yeah right.

The players are virtual prisoners at the hotel. 'It's like Fawlty Towers, man,' moans Paul. 'All there is is a pool table or table tennis.' Twice daily training sessions, back-to-back satellite TV, no distractions, no women, no sex. 'Dame Edna Everage is looking good to me right now, I'm telling you,' says Paul. Still he reflects: 'Instead of playing in the World Cup we could have been on holiday in Tenerife.' We both contemplate this for a moment. There but for the grace of God and all that. And at least the quiet offers plenty of time for career planning.

Paul and Fitzy have been split up, so that Fitzy, who is seen as something of a leader, can room with Walter Boyd, who has been let back into the squad.

When the Boyz flew to New York in May, to play their last warm-up match against the Caribbean All Stars, Blacka paid his own way to get on the same flight as the team and pleaded to be let back. He had gone to counselling sessions with Rev Al Miller, the team's chaplain, and had authored a contrite letter which was released to the Jamaican media. Yet Simoes was unrelenting. Later Boyd called the coach begging for a meeting. It was refused. Boyd turned up regardless, insistent. It was during that exchange, with Boyd at last in tears, that the tide finally turned. Simoes was to comment later: 'My God, more punishment than that, more humility I have never seen.' Boyd was a broken man. A vote was taken among the team on the flight home. He got fifteen votes for, six against – some thought, perhaps rather harshly, that the six were being honest and the others said 'yes' for an easy life. Simoes announced Blacka was to be given back his place on the bus. But a day before the World Cup, he is still not match-fit.

Lens, 14 June

Caribbean communities throughout England have been networking through businesses, radio stations, and word-of-mouth to promote the sale of World Cup packages.

The British marketing offensive is doing quite well generally. A two-man outfit called Parris and Bonaparte has volunteered for the job, one thin, the other thinner, with a snappy line in sharp suits. They have managed to drum up fairly hefty press coverage. Managing director of Joe Bloggs, Shami Ahmed, says he had the opportunity to sponsor the England team but turned it down. Oh really? The company's director Bushra Ahmed adds: 'We needed good-looking, trendy people to get involved with. The Reggae Boyz just fit the bill. They're already popular and they haven't really done anything yet.'

In Lens, judging by the number of white supporters wearing woolly hats with knitted dreadlocks attached, it seems as though anyone who has ever smoked a spliff, listened to reggae or holidayed in the Caribbean, feels eligible to join the Jamaican supporters' club.

Not in the least embarrassed by how much she has on show, through the crowd sashays a woman on platform rubber-soled slingbacks. Her hair, sculpted into a wavy black tower, announces her progress through groups of startled onlookers while the salivating hordes in her wake are captivated by her form. Long, solid brown legs finally arrive at very round hips, which nip into a tiny waist and then out again into a hoiked-up pair of large breasts stuffed into a black leather bra contraption. Encasing her body is an incidental piece of canary yellow micro-mesh net, intricately fashioned into an all-in-one hot-pant suit, with a collar. In a nod to decency she wears knickers not a thong. Having found her seat – four away from mine – she instead sits astride the concrete barrier and writhes up and down it. Men are rendered speechless with lust. Women nudge each other in disbelief. But no one pretends not to look.

The team, lined up for the Jamaican national anthem, look very new, quite scared. Well, they are beaten by Croatia 3-1. Robbie Earle wins a moment of glory for his sixteen years as a pro, with an equalising goal at the end of the first half. Pure energy circulates around the stadium, the celebrations last the whole of half-time. But for some reason, the second half is downhill all the way. As if terrified by their advantage, the team do nothing to maximise it. Next to the hulking Croats the players look tiny and as untogether as a mad woman on one of her madder days. Instead of a team, forged with the much-publicised discipline imported from Brazil, there is a group of individuals hell-bent on playing their own careerist game. And where oh where is Walter Boyd? Why doesn't Simoes put him on? Finally in the eighty-first minute of the match, he makes an appearance. He needn't have bothered.

As one man on the subdued Dover ferry says: 'We buried but we na dead yet.'

Afterwards, those who hadn't expected much from the 'Calypso Kings' are what you might call kind. The *Daily Mail* has this to say about Earle's equaliser: 'That goal remains the happiest of consolations for everybody's adopted World Cup infants.' Infants? The *Mirror* comments hastily: 'Party's over for the Reggae Boyz. The dreadlock holiday is over.'

Truth to tell it had been before the first whistle blew. Earlier, Horace Burrell had said, 'We're one big happy family. There are no problems in the camp.'

But he was wrong, Simoes wasn't happy. Before his team arrived in France, a row had erupted when his £210,000 government-funded salary – making him the highest paid public official in Jamaica – was exposed by the *Sunday Herald* newspaper. In response, in an open letter, Simoes had said he had 'no intentions of renewing my contract with Jamaica and with this country's money. I am becoming very frustrated for behaviour like this.'

And if Simoes was none too pleased, the team were in a right state before the Croatia match. Misguided, you could say, had been someone's idea to watch the documentary made by Trans World International. Big mistake. The crew had bought exclusive access to the team, filmed players at home, at their training camp in Jamaica, scenes of Fitzy laughing about how much money he was hoping to make through the team, and then a shot of his big new house. Fitzroy taking the piss out of amenities at the team house on camera was not appreciated. For a bunch of people who'd spent months in close proximity, over-tired and fretful, it was the last straw. So the night before their first match saw a team squabbling instead of in bed.

The programme's makers were escorted away from Chaumont after having made the mistake of showing their faces, but only after a lot of verbals with senior JFF members.

Reports of the upset reached Jamaica including the fact that Captain Burrell, and the gun he carries, were shown on the documentary.

The island's countless radio and television talk-ins were full of the news. It would not be overstating the case to say the majority of Jamaicans felt betrayed. Once more, it was felt that the island had been shown in a bad light. After the much publicised phenomenon of the gangster Yardies years ago and then Jamaica ER – a television series which revealed to British audiences shocking scenes of the violent end of poverty, at Kingston public hospital – it now seemed it was football's turn to be taken apart.

Brixton, Hinglan', 21 June

Prospects of going through to the next round are looking less than hopeful. Still, here in Rumours Wine Bar two DJs are set up in one corner, while two large-screen televisions wait for victory or at least a respectable show against Argentina.

They get it when the two sides have eleven men. Some order has been restored to the team. Goalie Warren Barrett does a highly efficient job against a barrage while Theodore Whitmore twice gets the ball off the feet of the enemy and Paul Hall, always a hard worker, clearly does not feel any worry about giving Lazio's Jose Chamot a hard time on the right wing. But a reluctance to mark their men, and giving the ball away too many times costs them. Daryl Powell's sending off is the turning point. They are mash up.

When Argentina's third goal is scored some of the crowd leave. But they do not go far, hanging around outside, relaying the unfolding tragedy via mobile phones. Peering in through the window when the pace warms up, the outsiders inch back in waiting for a miracle. It never comes and as a fifth goal slams into the Jamaican net, the despair is too much to bear. Two women walk out sobbing. One man called Patrick, who has travelled from Barking and sits alone throughout the match, looks close to breaking point. The DJ, in a desperate bid to raise the gloom, plays 'Don't Worry Be Happy' but Patrick's eyes fill up regardless.

'This is terrible.' His voice cracks. 'We had no possession of the ball, no discipline . . .' He looks down, shakes his head, unable to continue, then pushing his chair back abruptly, goes outside and stands weeping near a bin. The DJ drops Bob Marley's 'Everything's Gonna Be Alright' but someone forgets to tell Patrick.

On the island there has been a belief that Jamaica would win the World Cup. Unused to sporting failure, many Jamaicans, especially those who didn't know much about football, could not conceive of any other result.

Jamaica, 25-26 June

A fug of gloom has settled on the island. Reggae Boyz billboards for Kentucky Fried Chicken and Cable & Wireless are like the detritus from an aborted wedding. This game against Japan – if Jamaica win it – would be a Pyrrhic victory.

I had arrived the night before – alone this time. Alone in all senses of that word. I had been ripped off all around and was pissed off. Skint, borderline depressed and all round anxious about being in Jamaica alone. To cap it all, I was staying in some low-budget hotel I'd picked at random from a guide book. It had been a close call. Spend $250 a night at the Wyndham or save my money and take a chance. Clive, a driver I'd befriended on previous trips, was a welcoming face at the airport. He was so obviously concerned that I was travelling solo, it didn't help matters.

We arrived at the Sandhurst Hotel around midnight. We woke up the doorman who was snoring on a black vinyl Chesterfield. Black marble floor tiles, a big red shag pile rug, chipped gilt mirrors and some overgrown, yellowed silk flowers in vases constituted the decor. Clive told me the hotel had been a favourite with rock stars. That must have been some time ago. Handwritten signs by someone who'd perhaps been writing upside down, mentioned breakfast and demanded payment at check-in.

It was midnight, my depression had crossed the border. The room was dire. The ceiling, smeared in something the texture of porridge, the colour of split-pea soup, summed it up. Alone, except for a dead cockroach on the floor, I tried to summon up some optimism. I failed.

I wake up at 5.30. Upstairs, from the patio, is a jungly view of the Blue Mountains' foothills. Unseen birds flap and squawk, something rustles in a nearby breadfruit tree. Two slender grey cats curl around my chair legs. In this raw tranquillity, the incongruity of Jamaica having a football team playing in France seems even more stark. A couple comes to sit at the next table. They eye me uncuriously before starting to read the paper, she in a black leather disco cap turned to the front section, frowning; he concentrated on sport. Intermittently they sip on breakfast bottles of Red Stripe.

The Deck, a bar near New Kingston, caters to the white-collar suburbanites. 'Waggonists' – as in band wagon – is the contemptuous name given them by the early-day football supporters. Gathered one last time, for a £5 breakfast, by the 9 a.m. kick-off they've already started on the white rum albeit in lacklustre fashion. Before they come home the Reggae Boyz have obviously decided they have some unfinished business, in the form of spanking Japan. We all watch incredulous, vindicated, rapturous as Tapper Whitmore taps in his second goal of the match and Jamaican pride is salvaged.

A few tears flow, as do the drinks. Men who've skived off work, in the guise of attending 'meetings', clap each other on the shoulder, blow whistles and jig up and down. When the match ends it is 10.45 in the morning. But already there is a simmering rage of crushed hopes and bitterness.

VIII – Not a easy road

Kingston, 29 June

The Captain picks me up from the hotel in his Mercedes SLK. I've never ridden in one before. Secretly I want him to put his foot down, but instead he drives at a very sedate speed. He's been listening to the sports show on Irie FM. 'You don't mind if I listen do you?' No.

We drive out of New Kingston, he's going to take me to a fish restaurant by the sea. Once we get out of the city, under the stars, the night is black. The air conditioning is cold but it would be rude to say anything.

A caller has come on and is berating the English television documentary. 'So stupid,' says Burrell shaking his head.

Nobody on the island has actually seen the offending footage but everyone is offended. With my accent I am

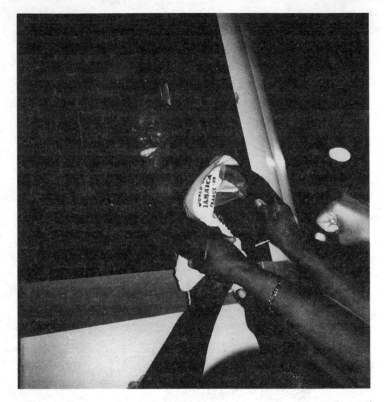

Tapper Whitmore, hero of Jamaica's victory over Japan is welcomed home.

viewed with suspicion. But not of course when I am with the Captain.

Over a bridge and down the other side we are at La Roose. He parks up, we're led into the empty restaurant. It's cubist, white concrete. During the day it must be wonderful, set right on the edge of the ocean. He chooses a table up on the platform, next to a plaster lion with a huge mane. By luck, or perhaps he asked for it, the sports show is playing through the speakers. He orders steamed fish for us.

Leaning forward, his chin in hand, he keeps nodding or tutting. And then he leans back, his cap off.

'Vital listening. For this job you must know what people are really thinking about and saying.'

The grouper arrives. It is enormous, covered in a thick sauce of okra and tomatoes. Then the fried bammy and our drinks, with the ice perspiring in the glasses.

Fans waited for hours at the airport to greet the players on their return from France.

It's delicious, firm, seasoned fish. The bammy is fried and crunchy with the tender okra for a while, and then, when its origins in cassava kick in, it's too filling. I eat half the fish and all the okra. The captain eats the lot and finishes before me, rubbing an appreciative hand over his filled belly.

Then he flirts. This happens all the time in Jamaica, where wooing women is considered sport. He wants someone to write his autobiography. Me, I think.

'I saw a picture of myself in a magazine in France and the eyes, my eyes . . .' he smiles in my direction. 'They had such vision in them. You know?'

I nod.

'I just felt looking at that picture that it said so much that it would make an excellent front cover for a book about me.'

The waitress comes to take our plates and remarks at what I've left. When she's gone, he leans over and pinches my spare tyre. He thinks he's being playful.

He talks about Bibi Gardner having been signed up to Bolton although just then he can't remember the club's name.

He leans back in his chair, the lion behind him.

Then he asks, 'Is it legal to write a book about anything you want?'

'What do you mean?'

'Well . . .' He searches for a delicate way to put this. 'People can just write about whatever they like in England?'

'Yes.'

He pulls a face and says 'Hmm.'

I get the impression, and not for the first time, that I am supposed to have offered to pay for access to the team.

An explanation at this point. In certain quarters, the Reggae Boyz became a product as their popularity ballooned. The first sniff of this fact came when TWI offered a substantial cheque to make their documentary. From that point the feeling was that foreign press should pay through the nose for anything other than the most superficial access.

We decide to leave. I lean back and he drives. As in the outer reaches of some cities in England they are developing shopping malls and fast-food places. Tastee, a patty chain, has opened another outlet. Burrell shows me the plot of land where he is going to have the latest in his own chain built, the Captain's Bakery.

A friend purrs alongside in a Mercedes, calls over and they talk, driving slowly side by side, about business and cars.

The friend says something about the size of Burrell's car, to which he replies, with a smile: 'It's good to drive something small now and then. It's got a lot of power.' Although I can't see him putting his foot down, not really his style.

The friend nods, then toots his horn and accelerates into the night. It feels a bit like being in an old-style movie with a rolling backdrop, driving along with the Captain. He talks about his ex-wife with whom he started the bakery and who now owns a chain specialising in cakes. He hasn't remarried, he says he likes to live alone, but he has a female companion who works for an airline. Most men I've run into in Jamaica are hot on female companionship.

Back in London I trawl through the newspapers to find coverage of the team's last match of the tournament. There is none bar one small paragraph in the *Mirror*. As far as Britain is concerned the Reggae Boyz chapter is over, their involvement in the first place a bit of a joke.

derby

HUNTER DAVIES

My appointment was at Derby County. J.B. Priestley, when he was roughly in this region, on his English journey, went to see a Derby match – but in the other sense of the word – Nottingham Forest versus Notts County. His comments about football, back in 1933, could almost be repeated today, word for word:

'Nearly everything possible has been done to spoil the game: the heavy financial interest; the absurd transfer and player-selling system; the lack of any birth or residential qualifications; the absurd publicity given to every feature of it by the press; the monstrous partisanships of the crowds.'

He didn't know the half of it, or the hundredth of it. In 1972, when I did a book about a year in the life of Tottenham Hotspur, football was very much as it was back in 1933, give or take a few price rises. Spectators mostly stood. Many of the stadiums were around 100 years old. There were no advertisements in the ground at Spurs, or at Arsenal, or in their programmes. That was considered rather vulgar. Top clubs were above such things. Shirts were virgin territory, unsponsored, unsullied by nasty commercial names or logos. There was no marketing and little money came in from merchandising or television. A First Division player in 1972 made £5,000 a year with a handful of top players getting £10,000 a year, about the same as in many other crafts and professions.

In the last ten years, almost everything in football has changed dramatically. The money, for a start. The average wage for an established senior player in the Premier League at the end of the millennium is £350,000. An England international will get around half a million and a super star one million a year, doubling that if he is suitably glamorous, willing to put himself about, posing and preening for advertisers and sponsors. Even at Derby County, not one of the more glamorous or wealthy clubs, most players, if they have decent careers, should be millionaires by the time they retire, with no need to work again for a living.

Then there is the racial mix. In 1972, when I did my Tottenham Hotspur book, there wasn't one black player in the team – and only one in the whole of the then First Division (Clyde Best of West Ham, born and brought up in Bermuda). Now around a third of professional footballers are black, far more proportionally than in the population as a whole.

Even more surprising has been the arrival of foreign players. When Priestley moaned about players not being qualified by birth or residence to play for their clubs, he was thinking of the apparent anomaly of Scotsmen playing for Arsenal or Geordies turning out for Manchester United. Never for a second was he thinking of real foreign johnnies playing for our famous clubs. There are now 150 non-British players in the Premier League, attracted by the huge wages, the relative freedom of contract and the enormous popularity and success of football in Britain among all classes and in most regions, as long of course as you are at or near the top, which in England means the Premier League.

Derby County is among the most English of English clubs, formed in 1884 by some members of the Derbyshire County Cricket Club, looking for a way to boost their income. They became one of the twelve original members of the Football League when it was formed in 1888. Yet today they are among the most foreign of English clubs. In 1998, they had at one stage eleven overseas players in their squad, drawn from a wide range of countries. They also have a brand new and most impressive stadium, Pride Park, opened in 1997, after 102 years at their old ground, the Baseball Ground.

But I wasn't going to see them play. You can get all that on the telly these days, five nights a week and twice on Sundays. I was going to watch them training at their handsome little training ground at Raynesway on the outer ring road of the city. In the car park I could see several Mercedes and BMWs, a sure sign of today's young professional footballer.

Out on the pitches, despite the foreign influx, I could hear all instructions and expletives being shouted in English, which of course is the basic language of football. Every player, everywhere, uses the same football words, as of course England gave football to the world, the rules and most of the language. And footballers, like spectators, are brought up in the same global village of football, using the same gestures and expressions.

Afterwards, in the training ground's dining room, there was much talk and banter about who had got that day's yellow bib. Bib as in training top, worn for practice matches. A yellow is awarded each day on a free vote to the person deemed worst at training – which means next day he'll have to wear it and suffer the appropriate mockery and ridicule. Footballers are very strong on ridicule, taking the piss, winding up their fellow players – all in good humour of course. So they think. Not so much fun for anyone who happens to be habitually picked upon.

On a central table were lined up a row of Derby County shirts, waiting to be autographed by the players, along with several footballs and giant-sized get well cards for children, all destined for worthy local causes and hospitals. Players, when they finished training, stood and dutifully signed their names on the items laid out, usually while still talking, still shouting. That scene hasn't changed in the last twenty-five years. It was the same at Spurs.

Igor Stimac was finishing his pasta and salad. Now that has changed. Most players were on chips and mushy peas, and they were all Brits. Stimac stood out as a mature figure among the younger players he happened to be sitting beside, many of whom appeared mere gawky youths. He is 6ft 2in, a tough, resolute defender, but he also has the aura of a senior prefect among school boys. Understandable. He is the team captain, and footballers, like school boys, live and work in hierarchies, with captains and senior players commanding respect. They also respect his intelligence, able to converse in several languages, an achievement well beyond the scope of most British players, and British persons, come to that. They also know that Igor has seen things, witnessed events, which they in their life, football or otherwise, are unlikely ever to experience.

'Pass the fucking juice then,' he said to one of the younger players across the table. I'd somehow not expected him to swear, as if his life might have put him above swearing, which was silly. A football club is an industrial setting, populated by working-class men, so they use the appropriate language, mostly without thinking. That's how a newcomer fits in. I remember going to see Kevin Keegan in Hamburg, when he had just joined them, and he was already swearing in German – but found he'd stopped swearing in English. He only spoke English at home, to his wife. And naturally, he didn't swear at her.

The juice was blackcurrant, poured from large industrial size cartons into jugs on each table. At Spurs, in the seventies, all they drank with meals, or in breaks from training, was tea, full of sugar. Igor asked if I'd like a tea, calling to a waitress behind a hatch to make me one, please.

When he'd finished his meal, we went into a little office, looking for a quiet place to talk, but the phone kept ringing. Actually, I said, I'd rather talk at your home, if you didn't mind. That would be more relaxing for you. Most interesting for me. Any chance of it?

With a well-known London or Manchester player, there would be little hope today of getting into their homes. Even getting ten minutes after training is hard enough as they are surrounded by agents and advisers, liable to demand money for interviews, or say their clients are too busy and have to rush off for something much more important, i.e. lucrative, such as opening a supermarket, doing some advertising, shaking some corporate hands.

'No problem,' said Igor, getting up. 'I'll just go and get changed.' He was wearing flip-flops with bare feet, T-shirt and jeans, having come straight from his post-training shower to the lunch table.

I stood waiting in the dining room and noticed Jim Smith, the manager, come out of his office. Football fans know him as the Bald Eagle, a jovial Yorkshireman in his late fifties who has seen many English clubs, as a player and manager. He was never a star as a player, nor has he himself played or worked abroad. Strange then he should have signed so many foreign players, but then that is where the bargains are today, if you are running a middle-ranking club.

He gave me a beam and a welcoming wave as he was talking to one of his coaches – something Bill Nicholson of Spurs would never have done if he'd spotted a stranger on his premises.

I'd rung the club a couple of days earlier, asking to see their captain, so presumably the request had gone through his office. He came over and shook my hand, said he'd read my book. Many years ago, of course.

I asked him about all the foreign players in his team, did they cause any problems. 'Oh not at all, they're all grand lads. The coaches find it more interesting, having players from different countries.' The different languages was not a problem either, thanks to Igor. 'He's the only one at the club who can speak Italian to our two Italians. And he can also speak Spanish to the South Americans.'

Settling them into a different culture, though, that must be a problem. I know that at the big London clubs it is normal for new players to spend months on their own, stuck in some anonymous hotel, feeling very lost and fed up.

'No problem here. One of our directors has a building firm, so they all move into one of his houses. The more foreign players I sign, the better his firm does. I should have been an estate agent, not a football manager . . .'

Igor got into his Shogun four-wheel drive – his Mercedes sports car was being serviced that day – and I followed behind in my Jag. Quite pleased it was a Jag, if four years old, and glad I'd got it cleaned. These things matter in football, if not in life. We drove for about fifteen minutes to the outskirts of Derby. He lives on a new estate in Littleover, at the end of an enclave of what looked like show houses, so new and sparkling they appeared unreal, like toy town houses. In this enclave live most of Derby's foreign players – which recently had included two Italians, two Costa Ricans, two Croatians, plus a Dane, Dutchman, Estonian and an Irishman.

The wives and children are in and out of each other's houses all the time, providing vital support for each other in a foreign land. Being a footballer's wife, foreign or otherwise, is not as glamorous as it might appear. It means living an unusual life, having plenty of money, but limited contact with the local community, liable to be uprooted at any time. Their husbands are with their team in a hotel usually one night a week, suffer extreme highs and lows, are unbearable when injured and, even when fit, don't have much energy or interest in the world at large.

Inside, his house looked as sparkling as outside, as if all the sofas and furnishings had just been unpacked that day. Igor's wife Suzana was at home when we arrived. She looks after everything domestic, does all the bills, organises their two young children. She made us coffee and laid out a large plate of biscuits and nuts, then went off in her car to pick up their children from school.

Igor was born in Croatia in 1967 in Metkovic, a small town of 20,000 on the border of what is now Bosnia though at the time, both Croatia and Bosnia were part of Communist Yugoslavia. His father was a director of the local electricity board, a responsible job, with a good salary but inflation was high and there wasn't much to spend money on. He has two brothers – one older, one younger. At school during the late seventies Igor carried a schoolbag emblazoned with the names of Keegan, Dalglish, McDermott – the whole Liverpool team in fact which then dominated England, and Europe. It was his older brother's bag, which Igor had inherited, but he was proud to carry it, as he loved football. He was always at school an hour before the bell rang in order to play football with his friends. He also collected Beatles records and had every LP.

He played for all the local youth teams and at fifteen was offered a place at a football school in Split, some hundred miles away, run by one of the country's two big teams, Hajduk Split. (The other Yugoslavian big team was Red Star Belgrade.) Several thousand boys passed through this school each year, many just on two- or three-week courses, but Igor was one of the 300 permanent pupils who received all their normal education, plus football training. 'It was the greatest football school in Europe. I remember when Ajax of Amsterdam were setting up their training school, they came to Split to see ours. Character training was as important as football training.'

PERFECT PITCH

Education and accommodation were free, but his parents had to send him pocket money. At the age of seventeen, two or three boys each year progressed to signing professional forms. Igor was one of them. 'There was no signing-on fee, which there is now. I was just so happy to be signed.'

He was paid according to a strict scale beloved of Communist countries, with three categories in which everyone was paid the same rate. The top category was for senior, which meant mostly international players. Then there were middle professionals and new professionals.

At eighteen, he hadn't made the first team squad, so he left for Dynamo Vinkovci, still in the first division, but a smaller club where he had a better chance of first team football. While there, he was picked for Yugoslavia's Under-21 team which went on to win the World Under-21 Cup in Chile in 1987.

'That was a marvellous team. We had players who are now world stars, like Suker, Boban, Jarni, Prosinecki, Mijatovic. I could have signed for a foreign club, after our success in Chile, but I'd always supported Hajduk Split, so I went back to them. I'd left them as a Small Door, as we say in Croatia. I returned as a Big Door.'

He became a regular in the Split side over the next six years which did well in Europe and he was made captain. 'In the last game of the 1990-91 season, just when the war started, we were in the Yugoslav Cup final against Red Star Belgrade. We beat them 1-0. Boksic scored. Seven days later, Red Star beat Marseille to win the European Champions Cup.'

Despite the war, and all the bombings, shootings, and ethnic killings, football somehow carried on. New leagues were established and Hajduk Split went into the newly formed Croatian league.

'It was our job, so we just got on with it. The crowds were a lot smaller, but people still wanted to watch football. When we travelled by coach to away matches, there would be road blocks, gunfire and fighting in the hills. On the way to play at Zador, the Serbs put bombs on the road to stop us, but they didn't go off. In one match, there was a bomb explosion on the terraces. The game was abandoned, but no one died. You couldn't escape the war, so you just lived with it. When the sirens went, you sheltered like everyone else.'

They also suffered like everyone else. Igor had an apartment, but for months on end there was no water or electricity and for a long time they were not paid. 'As captain, I had to go and complain on behalf of the players, which didn't make me popular with the club.'

Hajduk Split had always traditionally been a Croat club, but like most teams, they had a sprinkling of players from all regions. 'When the war began, we had a few Bosnians and Serbs. They were our friends, our colleagues. They wanted to stay playing with us, to earn their money, but they began to get warning letters, threatening them. In the end they went. Some of our younger players, the Croats, gave up football completely to go off and fight for Croatia.' So why didn't you?

'It was felt that the top players, the internationals, had a duty to carry on, play their best and be ambassadors for the country. When we played for Croatia, we were letting the rest of the world know that Croatia existed. It was very emotional, playing for Croatia in those early matches.'

After the first Croatian season finished in 1993, Igor felt it was time to leave. 'But it was the wrong time. No one wanted to come to Croatia and look at players. So I took the first offer that came along which was Cadiz, in the Spanish first division.'

Igor had got married in 1990 to Suzana whom he had met in a nightclub in Split when she was seventeen. She had been Miss Yugoslavia and become a model. Even in war-torn countries, footballers manage to live like footballers anywhere.

'Cadiz was a mistake. I hadn't realised how much they were struggling when I signed for them. They had sold their better players and we got relegated. Next season, we got relegated again. I was doing well playing for the Croatia national team – and we beat Spain 2-0 in a friendly in 1992 – but not well with my club team, so after eighteen months, I decided to come back to Hajduk Split.'

He stayed there for two years before Derby signed him in October 1995 for £1.5 million. 'I had signed for Vicenza in Italy but at the last moment, my club was not happy with the terms, and it fell through. That's when Jim Smith came along. He didn't come and see me play, but watched me on tapes.'

Igor had never been to England, though his wife had, competing in a Miss World contest in 1988. 'It was just as I expected. No surprises.' Oh come on. 'Well I knew all about English football, having followed it and watched it on television. Perhaps the people were a surprise. I had been told English people would be cold and unfriendly, but everyone has been warm and very kind. Perhaps because I'm a footballer. I don't know. I wasn't known here at all when I arrived. People didn't know me or anything about Croatia, even where it was.'

He had heard of Derby County, so he says, even though when he arrived they were languishing at seventeen in the First Division. 'We played Tranmere on my debut game. I scored but we got beaten 5-1. I wasn't depressed because I saw the quality and realised we could only get better. We were unbeaten for the next twenty games – and won promotion.' Now they are a respectable Premier League side, lying that day in seventh position.

He was then joined by a fellow Croatian, Aljosa Asanovic. 'I told Jim Smith about him, said he was my friend and he wanted to come to England. I said he was very experienced, who would do well for Croatia in Euro 96. He should look at him now, because afterwards his price will be much higher. He got him for only £960,000 just before Euro 96. He played well, so his price rose to £3 to £4 million.'

He finds the football here much more physical. In Croatia we pass the ball more, with more passes, keeping the ball. English players did not used to be so good technically as Europeans, but now I think they are.

'Footballers themselves are the same the world over. You get the jokers, the ones who moan, the ones who never spend any of their money, the ones who disappear the moment training is over.'

But he has found English social habits a bit different. At his first Christmas, there was a team party which started at two, after training, and by four, he'd had more than enough to drink. All the British players were still pouring down the beer, pint after pint, hours and hours later.

'I still don't know how they do it, how they have such

a capacity. After a couple of glasses of wine, a normal footballer in Europe on a night out will think now, where can I get a nice shag, or where should I go for a nice meal. In Britain, they just think where should we go to keep on drinking. It's amazing.'

The training system is also different in England, though with more European managers arriving, this is beginning to change. 'We still don't train in the afternoons at Derby, which we did at Split and in most of Europe. A game is normally on a Saturday afternoon, so if you are used to training in the afternoon, the body's metabolism is ready for it.'

In Split, they did three whole days of training, plus two afternoons. So is football here easier, with less training?

'Not at all. We play more matches in England, so that leaves less time for training. But England is getting more like Europe all the time. Since I've been here, the gaffer has hired a club psychologist, which Derby didn't have before, and two more physiotherapists who look after things like diet and fitness. And we've got our brilliant new stadium, which I never expected when I came. I couldn't have chosen a better time to come. The set-up at Derby is now as good as most places in Europe.

'One of the nicest things that happened was during Euro 96. The club shop bought 500 Croatian shirts, all because of my connection. They were for the fans to buy – and they were all sold out in a matter of days.

'People still don't know much about Croatia, but they know we exist. Your politicians were not helpful. They supported the Serbs when they were killing our people. When I explained the true story to ordinary people, then they understood. Most people in England are very insular.

You think anything of importance in the world only happens here. I suppose other people think that as well. We have a thousand islands in Croatia, and when you visit any of them, the people there have no idea what's happening in the rest of the world.'

There was the shouting of children in the front hall. Suzana had arrived home, bringing Mia, aged two-and-a-half, and Luka, their seven-year-old son who went straight up to his bedroom to change out of his school clothes. Mia had brought home a little Danish girl with incredibly blonde hair, daughter of another Derby player. She asked Igor, ever so politely, and in perfect English, if she could have a biscuit. Igor said yes, of course. Mia got out a children's video and asked her father to put it on – speaking to him in Croatian. He replied in English, saying she could do it herself, just work it out.

Igor couldn't speak English when he arrived. Now he is fluent. During our conversation, there had not been the slightest hesitation with any words or ideas. The only confusion had been mine when I asked if he had an agent and he said no, he used Encounter. I said that firm was new to me. Later on, his mobile phone rang and when he put it down he said: 'That was my encounter.' I then realised he'd meant accountant.

'When I arrived, I thought I would be able to say a few words of English, as I'd done some English at school, but I couldn't understand one word.'

Presumably Derby laid on some intensive tuition, along with the lovely house on the lovely estate?

'No. I've had no lessons or tutors. I picked a lot of my English up from television. I found that movies were the best. They speak more slowly and it's clear in most situations what they must be saying. But it's mostly due to speaking English all the time at work. As captain, I come off the pitch exhausted as much by talking as by playing.'

His mobile phone rang again. It was a woman this time, the mother of the little Danish girl. 'Let me see my dear,' he said in very posh English. 'I think she's still here. I'll go and see.'

Their two children speak English without a trace of an accent, but at home with their parents they speak Croatian. Every evening, Suzana gives them Croatian lessons, so they learn it properly, including the grammar.

'Luka will often use certain English words when he is speaking Croatian to us – technical terms, to do with the video or computer, which he doesn't known in Croatian. He also uses English words like "Monday", to save him thinking of the word in Croatian. But no, he's not confused. He knows when he's speaking which language.'

They are pleased with the children's progress at school, where they seem very happy. I said it will be a great help, wherever they go in the future, having learned fluent English. 'What matters is that they grow up to be good people,' said Igor, solemnly, 'who respect others and respect themselves.'

Suzana's own English was better than Igor's when they arrived, so she says. She couldn't actually speak it, but she remembered more of the grammar. She has picked up a lot from watching Oprah Winfrey on television, but her English is a bit more hesitant than Igor's. She doesn't have the constant practice, stuck at home on her own for most of the day.

Igor acquired his Spanish while in Cadiz. As for his Italian, he has never lived or worked there, but his part of

Croatia is near Italy and he often went there shopping or on holiday. 'I just picked it up.'

They both love their English house. 'Anything in England would have seemed wonderful to us, coming from a war zone like Split,' said Igor. The house, four beds, with a large garage, cost them only £125,000, bought at a discount through the club's director. Even so, the price seemed very low compared with similar houses favoured by London footballers. Dennis Bergkamp, for example, lives in a new estate north of London which cost him £650,000. (I know the price because a journalist friend, Richard Littlejohn, lives in the same street.)

Suzana says she likes almost everything about her life here, even more than in Split. 'I see more of Igor in England. He is home every day at two o'clock, after his training. In Split, I hardly saw him. It wasn't just the longer training, but every five minutes he was off somewhere, meeting friends, football people, doing things, doing business.'

Igor has no business interests in England, though he would be willing to consider any offers or suggestions. Derby County is not a very fashionable team, nor are they in a large conurbation, so the chances of promotional work are limited. But back in Croatia, he is a veritable entrepreneur.

'I bought my first discotheque in Split eighteen months ago. It's called Mississippi. Yes, in English. My two brothers look after it, and we try to go for most of the summer. Recently I started another club and restaurant, which I built myself. It's on an island called Brac in the town of Bol. This is where the young and rich go, the jet set of Croatia. Oh yes, we have them. The club is called

"Faces" and can hold 4,000 people. It's been a big success. Next I'm going to buy a hotel in Split.'

He got out holiday brochures for the island of Brac and it looked wonderful, with white beaches and a perfect sea, more Caribbean than Adriatic. One day, he will go home to live in Croatia, but in the immediate future, he sees himself at Derby.

'I have a two-year contract. I have given Derby my heart, so why should I change? I am happy here. The fans like me. The atmosphere at all English matches is brilliant, far better than Europe. I am proud to be the captain. I am a strong character and I like to be leader. I like to be positive and support players, do the best for the lads.

'I've been lucky. This is a great time for football in England. Everything is booming. And it will get even better. I think in five years, players will earn ten times what they get now.'

Ten times? But they're getting so much already. 'Well, even more than they are now. But this is definitely the best time to be in English football.'

What happens then, after Derby? 'I might have a final year playing for Hajduk Split. Then at thirty-three I'll retire. I don't want to keep playing when I'm past it. I don't want the crowd shouting "Go Home".

'I might then go into coaching. I want to stay in football, so if a coaching job came up, in Croatia, England, or anywhere, I would be interested. I want to help young players to do what I've done.'

During his four years in England so far, he's seen a lot of English football, watching every possible match on television, reading the football pages in the *Express*, *Mail* and *Telegraph*, but he hasn't seen much of Britain. Their only family trip has been to Alton Towers, which is not far away. They haven't yet been to Stratford, the Lake District or Scotland. Igor shrugged and said he hasn't got much energy left after training. He'd also had a back injury for the last ten weeks. When not training, he was supposed to be resting.

But he and his wife did have a day in London, not long after they arrived. 'We went on the Tube, visited the Tower, saw Big Ben, Trafalgar Square, Piccadilly. London's not a British town really. It's a cosmopolitan world city. It would take a month to get round it. I'm glad I'm not at a London club. I like Derby. It's easy getting to the training ground and the club.'

Suzana said she liked Derby as well and was very fond of the Eagle shopping centre. I made a face. Coming from Split, any modern shopping centre must seem pretty wonderful. When going out in Derby, to a restaurant or a cinema, they don't get pestered much by fans. 'Well, people might shout "Hi Igor", but they are all nice people. At a place like Man Utd, the players must be under a lot more pressure all the time.'

The only thing they don't like is the traffic. Derby and Split are similar in population, each around 200,000, but there is no comparison in traffic. 'There is so much here, so many hold-ups.'

Nor do they like the weather. 'In Split, we have 300 days of sun a year. Here it's more like three days. In the winter, you are stuck indoors all the time. In Croatia, we live our life outside.'

Suzana cooks at home in the Croatian style, which she says is much healthier. 'I buy the same food from the same places as everyone else, but we eat a lot of vegetables and fish, rather than meat. I cook them in the Croatian way.' I couldn't quite follow what the difference was, except she always uses olive oil in salads.

'Life in England is very easy,' she said. 'Everything is easy. But then things are always easy, if you have money . . .'

Very true. There seems little doubt that Igor will end up with a lot of money when he does retire, though in the summer of 1998 he didn't manage to spend much time with his investments back in Croatia. He was otherwise engaged in France, the backbone of Croatia's team which stuffed Germany 3-0, beat Romania 1-0 and ended up third in the World Cup, with his friend and colleague Davor Suker winning the Golden Boot for scoring the most goals. We won't talk about England, who got eliminated much earlier. Igor has done pretty well, for a foreigner in our land.

Taken from London to Loweswater *by Hunter Davies, to be published by Mainstream, £14.99, in September.*

the people's party's game

Football has never had so many political supporters. And almost all of them are from the Labour Party.

All Labour MPs want it known that they support the local lads. Peter Mandelson told his local paper it was 'so important' for his constituents that Hartlepool avoid relegation last season. Meanwhile, Tony Benn claimed in 1997 that workers across the country should support his constituency team Chesterfield in their FA Cup run, as they represented the fight against the establishment. Neither man has been noted for his commitment to the game. Indeed, Mandelson's only other known comment about it, when as Trade Secretary he instantly found himself in the middle of BSkyB's proposed take-over of Manchester United, was a near perfect definition of the Third Way. He said: 'I love football and am a great supporter of those who broadcast it.'

Mandelson and Benn were following their leader, who had famously allied himself with Kevin Keegan's then sexy team. You may remember the party conference between Euro 96 and the 1997 election when Blair played keepy-uppy with the Newcastle manager and adapted the Skinner and Baddiel anthem to predict that Labour was coming home.

It would take a superhuman effort not to be cynical

about these Labour antics. But there is more to them than might appear. Contrary to popular opinion, not all politicians are always trying to get you to look them in the eye so you don't notice them stealing the wallet from your pocket. Most at least start out like regular human beings. Or that's my experience. Perhaps I would say that, as I have grown up in the Labour Party. After university, I worked for two years in the head office as chair of National Labour Students, later becoming adviser to John Prescott. Then, after spending a few years making TV programmes about politics, I joined the BMP advertising agency and managed Labour's campaign for the last election. I am even prepared to accept some of the blame for Labour's attempts to associate with football. For instance, I was responsible for the party political broadcasts before the election, including the biography of Tony Blair which gave us our one chance to choreograph private insights into the man's character. It began with him revealing that as a child he certainly didn't want to grow up to be a politician – that seemed too boring. Instead, he said, he had wanted to be a professional footballer.

Mea culpa. There's no point in pretending that Labour's rhetoric doesn't contain a strong strand of populism. 'Football is the new rock and roll. Embrace, embrace,' the advertisers might preach to politicians. 'In this age of media intrusion, get yourself a hinterland and a rounded private life. Go for football – it's more marketable than opera.'

And it is in the nature of politicians, who work very long hours over many years with single-minded dedication, to have little time left for families, let alone a social life or hobbies. Often, football is all they know outside their work.

For many of them do enjoy the game. It was little noticed that at last year's party conference Blair limped up to the rostrum to give his speech, thanks to an injury sustained a few days before in a bad tackle by one of the Special Branch detectives assigned to protect him. Blair has organised many matches at the Prime Minister's residence at Chequers which have included his sons, Prince William, Lionel Jospin and a squad of policy advisers.

Alastair Campbell, Blair's spokesman, spent most of his Cambridge University days playing the bagpipes around Europe at Scotland games and travelling to Burnley matches. Now he works in one of the most pressured jobs in Britain, but somehow he still manages to sneak off every week and I've bumped into him with his children at the most unlikely grounds. We at BMP gave him a special edition poster to celebrate the election victory: an updated version of the campaign slogan – 'Britain Just Got Better' – decked out in Burnley's claret and blue colours. It now hangs on his office wall in Downing Street.

In fact, there are plenty of genuine supporters – fanatics even – on Labour's benches. If they were not MPs, these are people who would gladly travel miles to a second-round League Cup match – without shouting about it from the rooftops. When MPs would normally do anything to be seen putting their own voters first, many are happy to be known to support unfashionable teams far from their constituencies. For instance, in the 1992-93 season, Peter Snape, member for the then marginal seat of

West Bromwich East, was chased out of the Hawthorns by Baggies directors after they lost 5-1 to Stockport County. Snape has supported County since childhood and ten years earlier had used up much personal political capital by leading the campaign to prevent the closure of Edgeley Park just before its centenary.

Credible support is not confined to northern men. When I was chair of National Labour Students in the late 1980s, only two people were keen to speak at the poorly attended meetings I organised to discuss the politics of football with Rogan Taylor, then from the Football Supporters' Association. One was Tom Pendry, the other Kate Hoey, whose love of Arsenal had led her from enthusiast to employee. Before entering Parliament, she ran lifestyle courses at Highbury, White Hart Lane and Stamford Bridge, advising young players on how to cope with everything from completing tax forms to ordering wine in restaurants. Hoey's enjoyment of Arsenal's victory in the 1993 FA Cup final was interrupted by a call from John Smith telling her she was sacked from the Opposition front bench. And when Michael Thomas, one of those under her tutelage, was scoring the last-minute Championship winner at Anfield in 1989, she was fighting the Vauxhall by-election which took her to Westminster. 'I wasn't allowed the evening off,' she recalls, 'but Michael lived in my constituency. We changed the campaign slogan to "The Winning Team" – with posters featuring Michael and me.'

You could say that was a dash of opportunism. But not many would argue it was exploiting the game, because she has such a long track-record. Hoey, Snape, Campbell and many others are, first and foremost, fans. They just happen to have jobs in politics. Some of their colleagues would even have preferred to keep their own enthusiasm private, because for one reason or another football has restricted their political climb. Take the Scottish MP who – despite Tony Blair's rule that Labour MPs should not be seen in France during the World Cup to avoid looking like queue-jumping free-loaders, and despite the government talking tough against touts – was discovered in a Glasgow car park handing over £500 in used notes, in the customary brown-paper envelope, for a ticket to Scotland's opening game against Brazil. This incident consigned him to a career of anonymity on the backbenches after an investigation by the Whips.

Before last summer's reshuffle, Brian Wilson was a high-flying minister in the Scottish Office. A former football journalist who loves Celtic, he wrote the centenary history of the club. Last spring, he got permission from the Whips to miss a late-night vote in the Commons saying he absolutely had to attend a meeting about a sectarian disagreement near his constituency. Unluckily for him, as several Scottish Whips settled down together after the vote to watch the Celtic–Rangers game on TV from their office in Parliament, the cameras zoomed in on Wilson in the crowd while the commentator noted the growing popularity of football attendance among Labour MPs. The Scottish Whips decided they no longer wanted to deal with Wilson, and so he is now a trade minister.

The hapless new MP for Hammersmith and Fulham, Iain Coleman, had worse luck. When his assistant, Dominic McElroy, left for a new job, he wrote a memo to his successor detailing how to run the MP's office. It included practical information about what time Parliament sits each day, how to use the House of Commons library and where to get a copy of *Hansard*. As the memo was inadvertently sent to the *Evening Standard*, we know that it also included other tips. McElroy wrote: 'Iain will not miss any Arsenal games for whatever reason. Clear diary, use whatever excuse necessary. Childcare is a good one, important vote at House of Commons (midweek games only), weddings, funerals, family events, etc.' As Bill Shankly might have put it, for Coleman football was much more important than a parliamentary career.

The dilemma of having divided loyalties can surface at the most inconvenient moments, as it did when Mike Gapes stood for selection as MP for Ilford South. At the final meeting of a hard-fought campaign he was asked a simple question by an opponent. 'Would I prefer Labour to win the next election or West Ham to win the League?' he repeated, buying time. All those about to vote knew he had wanted to be an MP for years, but also knew he had been a season ticket-holder for even longer. He tried a cute answer: 'Well, we've had Labour governments in the past.' He was selected.

Because there is a depth of football support within Labour, football rhetoric plays well inside the party as well as outside it. On the morning of Wednesday 11 May 1983, a hopeful thirty-year-old lawyer rang John Burton, the secretary of the Trimdon Village Branch of the Sedgefield Constituency Labour Party, to ask if he could be considered as the parliamentary candidate. It was only a month before the general election and Sedgefield, a safe seat, was the last place in the country to select its Labour MP.

Burton told him to come round to his house that night as five of the most important local party members would be there anyway. At 9 p.m., Tony Blair knocked on Burton's door. He was ushered in and told to sit quietly while they finished watching the European Cup-Winners' Cup final. 'He said he quite liked football,' says Burton. 'Whether he was being polite or not I don't know.'

The game ended 1-1 and Blair had to wait for extra time before Alex Ferguson's Aberdeen lifted the Cup. Paul Trippett remembers: 'He sat there, watched the match, took part in the conversation guys have when the match is on, you know, "good shot", "bad cross", so he was one of the guys.' After the game, the five quizzed Blair about his politics but Peter Brookes recalls thinking only: 'Why on earth should we give a nomination to this bloke who's just arrived and spoiled the football?' History records that Blair was duly selected and that Alex Ferguson attended the first Labour Party Conference after the 1997 election.

Blair's selection gave birth to the idea of football as a contacts sport for Labour. It now plays a part in the complex networking activities of many Labour people. For anyone eager to ingratiate themselves with the party hierarchy – wannabe MPs, journalists, civil servants – football has become for Labour what golf is to businessmen: an ideal place to relax, chat and deal. Evidence of this is the number of tickets doled out by parliamentary lobbyists. 'There is a high demand for football tickets among Labour MPs, many companies buy private boxes at stadiums across the country, ergo senior business executives are able to enjoy the football on a Saturday afternoon in the company of a key contact,' explains Aleks

Szczerbiak, a former lobbyist who used to entertain MPs in Vauxhall's box at Luton Town.

The bait doesn't always catch the intended fish, though. After an invitation to an England game in Euro 96 was sent to the home of a Labour MP, his young son rang to say that although his dad was out of the country for a month he was sure he would want at least a couple of tickets.

In 1990, a team of male and female advisers to Blair and other rising stars like Brown, Straw and Blunkett started arranging a weekly kick-about. 'It began as a social thing,' says James Purnell, now an adviser to the Prime Minister. 'We were all scattered around Parliament and this was a way to make sure we got to know each other.'

However, the football quickly became more important than the social thing. Regular training was organised, a team called 'Red Menace' was established and weaker players were left on the touchline. Political animals are intensely competitive and any disagreements between them during the week started to show on the field, with tackles going in hard and sendings-off not uncommon. The kick-about turned really serious just before the last election when Purnell entered the team in an FA league under the name of 'Demon Eyes' – a reference to the Conservatives' poster attacking Tony Blair. As no women are allowed to play in men's football under FA rules, it has led to accusations of chauvinism.

Helen Wilkinson, a founder of Demos, regularly described as Blair's favourite think-tank, recently wrote a high-profile attack on New Labour's 'new lad' culture. 'The problem,' she argued, 'is that "team bonding" too readily turns into male bonding. The old boys' network may have progressed from golf to football but the fundamental rules are the same.'

In fact, the problem is that for some people the football came first. They had played at school and would have joined the team of any company they worked for. They just happened to be in a political team. When the game became mixed with the business of developing contacts, there was a conflict of priorities.

Where there is a shared love of football, that conflict does not arise. Business and pleasure then mix together perfectly, which is why so many MPs and journalists travel to matches with each other, even to support opposing teams. While he was political editor of the *Mirror*, Alastair Campbell periodically went with Peter Snape to Burnley–Stockport games. On the way to one, Snape was called on his car-phone to be tipped off that Michael Heseltine was soon to be recalled to Major's government after years on the backbenches under Thatcher. Between them, Snape and Campbell compiled an exclusive front-page splash which was filed to the *Mirror* before they even reached the ground.

Naturally, this relationship works both ways. As soon as Tony Blair was elected Labour leader in 1994, Campbell crossed sides and went to work for him as chief press spokesman. The most controversial element of their pre-election press strategy came to a conclusion on Saturday 15 March 1997 at the unlikely setting of the Brentford FC ground. It was at Burnley's away game that Campbell bumped into Stuart Higgins, then editor of the *Sun*. The following Tuesday, the biggest circulation tabloid in the country abandoned its twenty-year loyalty to

the Conservatives by splashing its front page with 'The
Sun Backs Blair'. Of course, there had been three years of
hard work put into getting that headline, but the friendship between Campbell and Higgins built up at scores of
Burnley games certainly did no harm.

Since then, football has started to help oil the wheels
of government. Terry Burns, the most senior civil servant
at the Treasury, was sidelined and forced to retire because
he did not get on with Gordon Brown. The *Financial Times*
began its profile of Burns' successor by explaining that he
was 'a football fan and a supporter of Tottenham Hotspur'. City analysts were told this was the most salient fact
about Andrew Turnbull because 'it will endear him to
Chancellor Gordon Brown's blokeish inner circle of
advisers and ministerial colleagues'.

Brown himself is a proper Scotland fan, his former
special adviser, Charlie Whelan, a regular at Spurs, a
present adviser at Norwich. His once closest ministerial
colleague, Geoffrey Robinson, is Labour's nearest thing to
Silvio Berlusconi: although he likes to make his money
offshore, his football is enjoyed much closer to home – he
owns a large stake in Coventry City in his constituency.
Helen Wilkinson may be right that this must make it very
difficult for people not interested in football to break into
those networks. But football can hardly be blamed for
that. Declaring an interest in the game may have lots of
political advantages. The point is that for many they are a
consequence, not the cause, of going to matches. These
advantages are comparatively new. While there have
always been Labour backbenchers sipping Bovril on a
rainy Saturday afternoon, they never thought of it as
anything more than fun. Some higher profile names even

became publicly linked with a team, Michael Foot with Plymouth Argyle and Roy Hattersley with Sheffield Wednesday for example, but this came simply from a love of their teams. They were innocent.

During Brian Walden's service as a Labour MP for inner Birmingham constituencies between 1964 and 1977, it had never occurred to him to tell any of his parliamentary colleagues, let alone a journalist, that he followed a team. It was only five years ago, when I produced his current affairs series for London Weekend Television, that I discovered he possessed an amazing memory for football trivia and had been a regular at Highbury since the 1940s.

He was one of the many public figures who started citing an interest in football at the beginning of the 1990s, stimulating media probing about which clubs they supported. During a round of promotional interviews for a forthcoming series of *Walden*, I was watching from the studio of a live LWT chat-show when he correctly identified in sequence the full names of all eleven of the Arsenal side which lost the 1952 FA Cup final 1-0 to Newcastle. I was impressed – he had got only ten in the rehearsal, after which I had rung the LWT library to confirm the right-back as Walley Barnes.

Until recently, football, like having a mistress, was a very private indulgence for politicians. In Susan Crosland's loving biography of her late husband, she wrote that watching Grimsby Town was a relaxing corner of Anthony Crosland's life which had 'nothing to do with his work' as Labour MP or foreign secretary.

When the pre-Blair Labour Party did try to harness football, it usually failed. It was clumsy and, I like to think, ahead of its time. The second most successful populist in Labour's history, Harold Wilson, never too shy to stand next to a Beatle in front of a photographer, asked: 'Have you noticed how we only win the World Cup under a Labour government?' But he was rebuked by Sir Stanley Rous for contriving to be photographed with the winning team.

In 1979, a local party agent put up posters in parts of Islington which said 'Arsenal for the Cup and Labour for the election'; not surprisingly, Spurs fans were not impressed. And in 1988, I put together a magazine called *Red* for National Labour Students with David Rocastle at his peak on the cover and interviewed across several pages inside. It was not a bestseller and instead of being the launch issue of a regular magazine, it turned out to be a one-off.

Football works for Labour now partly because politics has changed. Crosland and Foot would have thought it ridiculous and superficial to advertise their fandom, but these days the media and the public want to know more about the habits than the beliefs of their MPs.

Perhaps more important, football has changed too. The British game has been reborn since Gazza's tears, and nobody is quicker to put its finger on the clitoris of the nation than Labour leaders. And football is essential to New Labour's new patriotism. It is crucial to Blair to be patriotic, partly because Old Labour's unilateralism looked anti-patriotic and partly because he is vulnerable to accusations that he may give up the pound and has already given Scotland and Wales their own parliaments. So the party has thrown its weight behind England's bid to host the World Cup, and Blair is quoted in support of

England before every big game. This is safe, because being a football patriot is less confrontational to our partners in Europe and elsewhere than other kinds of flag-waving.

North of the border, support for the Scotland team helped rally enthusiasm for national identity and combat the Scottish Nationalists' charge that Labour was essentially English. The effect has been so powerful that when Adam Ingram, the Member for East Kilbride but a Minister in the Northern Ireland Office, this summer proposed the controversial early release of paramilitary prisoners as part of the peace process, he was the only Scottish Labour MP in the Commons. He rose to make his speech at 4.30 p.m., the precise moment Brazil kicked off the opening game of the World Cup against the Tartan Army, and nobody with a hint of self-preservation would have wanted it known they didn't care. In fact, two-thirds of them were anxious for the media to report that they had defied Blair and travelled to France for one or more of Scotland's matches.

However, populism is an art, which some have mastered and some have not. Let's give the biscuit to Tony Banks. Certainly not to Joan Walley, proud supporter of Port Vale, the team in her constituency. In eleven years as an MP, her most extensive national press coverage came at the start of the 1994-95 season when she complained that Manchester United were insulting her voters by sending a youth team to Vale Park for a Coca-Cola Cup match. Unfortunately for her, it turned out her voters had been privy to a treat. Not only were John Rudge's side well-beaten, but twelve months later Messrs Beckham, Butt, Scholes and the Nevilles were part of the team that won the Double. That is an exception. As a rule, New Labour's media management is exemplary. And without a reserve of genuine credibility, they knew they couldn't have even tried to capitalise on the growing popularity of the game. Without it, sudden support would have looked crass. So New Labour politicians have bolstered their authenticity by dredging up past commitments. Gordon Brown boasts of having been behind the goal when Scotland's David Narey scored against Brazil in the 1982 World Cup in Spain, before he became an MP.

Part of the beauty of football for Labour is that they will always use it better than anyone else. The Tories (remember them?) are still the party of rugby and cricket, and there is no Conservative MP in the Parliamentary XI. There is a reason why John Major claimed his proudest moment was being admitted as a member of the Marylebone Cricket Club. Never mind Downing Street, entering the all-male Long Room was the apogee of the establishment for the boy from Brixton.

Most Conservative MPs who claim to like football admit to the cardinal sin of following more than one team, and even the most genuine can appear like recent converts. Major over-reached himself by suddenly popping up on Radio 5 Live with half-time comments, and David Mellor is derided with accusations that he deserted Fulham for Chelsea. On the front cover of *When Saturday Comes* in April 1992, the month before the general election, there was a close-up photo of Major and Mellor in the Stamford Bridge directors' box, with a speech bubble from Mellor asking, 'Do you come here often?' and one from Major replying, 'Only in election year.' It is a mistake that Labour politicians find easy to avoid.

i killed 'pulpa' etchemendi!

DANIEL SAMPER

There are some who believe the job of a football director is easy: appearing in the press and on TV, smoking cigars, getting free tickets for all the games, wearing a tie at the stadium, greeting one's international colleagues with a kiss on the cheek, and staying at the best hotels on the club's expenses. Clearly such people have never been football club directors!

My passage through the tough world of football bosses was practically the result of a twist of fate and lasted a very short time: a mere eight years, which is nothing compared to the average staying stint of a football chief, which is in fact sixty-seven and a half years.

I was a member of the board of directors of the Club Independiente de Santa Fé, in Bogotá, Colombia, knowing nothing about finances, hardly anything more about football, and more to my credit having hardly ever worn a tie except on two or three occasions which included my own First Communion and an uncle's appointment as Minister of Agriculture.

How was it that a twenty-seven-year-old popular satirical columnist landed on the board of directors of a football club? Fandom. Pure and simple fandom. The same sort that has driven other human beings to risk their own lives or to attempt against that of others. Ever since I was a kid I have been a supporter of Santa Fé, the club which in 1948 became the first professional football champions in my country. Among other details, Santa Fé copied its glorious uniform from Arsenal FC and hired Charles Mitten and George Mountford, the first English players to have stepped onto Colombian grass.

Having won the national championship five times between 1948 and 1971, Santa Fé had settled comfortably into lesser positions, and was just as likely to lose to the club at the bottom of the league as to beat the top one. Though if the truth be told, the possibility of losing to both was higher than that of a double victory. As a Santa Fé follower, on many a bitter Monday I slipped into my column of political and social commentary some criticisms of the players, the manager and the directors. I should also admit that, when we won, I would hum victorious songs smugly from my corner of the editorial page, to the outrage of my nineteenth-century readers.

One day the president of the club called me and said in an irritated tone of voice: 'Seeing as you're so full of advice in your column, I will offer you a golden opportunity to turn your Santa Fé into champions. I have a vacant place on the board of directors and I want you to take it.'

The President, Guillermo Cortes, had been elected to the post not just because he was an avid fan, but because he knew about finances. One worrying signal about his mental health is the fact that ever since he was a boy he has been nicknamed 'La Chiva' (a goat, as in 'crazy as a goat'). His friends, all of us who adore him, still know him by that name.

'I know nothing about finances, I hardly know anything about football, and I've never been a member of a board of directors,' I apologised.

'Here, you will have nothing to do with the balance sheet, you will be concerned with the club's image.'

'Besides,' I said, 'my religious principles prevent me from wearing a tie.'

'Terrific,' he replied. 'The players will love a director who dresses like them.'

And that is how I became a part of Santa Fé and the bizarre world of football bosses. Very soon I was to experience the problems which afflict a director. For me they started when I suggested adopting a mascot that would symbolise the fierceness of our team, and they ended when I killed 'Pulpa' Etchemendi.

Between the first and the last there were many incidents. I will not now go into, for reasons of good taste, the moments of bizarre anguish we underwent on the eve of the club's first participation in the Libertadores Cup of 1980. An unknown infection – perhaps planted by our opponents – attacked the stomachs of our boys, turning them into rag dolls. I have often related in specialised medical journals the varied efforts of the therapies we tried to battle against the intestinal disintegration of the team, and the proven inefficiency of traditional cures such as rice water, cinnamon infusions, a pinch of salt on the navel, and a cocktail of aniseed and Lomotil.

I will only say that looking back on it now it seems diarrhoea can act as a stimulant for fast forwards because that night Alberto Santelli, who was barely five feet seven inches tall, scored two headers against an Ecuadorian side. Nor will I mention here the delicate labour of marriage counselling we often had to undertake in the board room when players from our side went AWOL from their saintly homes for weeks, following the footsteps of vacuous and tempting women who had nothing to offer them except the delicacies of easy sex, insatiable passions and turgid flesh. Almost nothing . . .

But I do believe the time has come to reveal what happened during two very difficult – even tragic – episodes I was involved in after fate, fandom, adventure and 'Chiva' Cortes turned me into a sports director for eight years.

A lion in the backyard

The problem of the lion started in early 1975. Convinced that every team needs a symbol to attract fans, I proposed to the board that we get a lion as Santa Fé's mascot. My colleagues approved this with enthusiasm, and with the same enthusiasm they put me in charge of finding one and bringing it to the house that was the club's headquarters, where it would have a special habitat.

Here I feel compelled to explain that had this task been instructed to the director of a Kenyan football club there would not have been much to it: simply go out into the fields with a piece of rope and a piece of meat, tie up the first lion that approaches to eat the meat, and take it to the club. In Colombia it's a little bit more complex because the only lions you can find in the streets are the rivals of the Rotarians.

In spite of this I was willing to show that journalists aren't only able to impart criticism, that we are also capable of doing things. I was imaginative: in my search for a cub I got in touch with the zoos all over Colombia, and with many circuses too. Weeks went by without a positive response. Until one day the hoped-for telegram arrived: in the zoo of Risarelda, in the region where the best coffee in the world is harvested, some baby lions were due to be born in May.

We immediately got in touch with the zoo's director, an understanding man who was also desperate due to the high birthrate among his lion population, and he agreed to sell us a cub for a symbolic fee.

'Monaguillo' was born on 13 May of the aforementioned year. After three weeks a friend and myself went on a journey to get him. It wasn't easy to get him into the jeep and to convince him that he was heading for a glorious destiny of fame, and not towards the melancholy of another dungeon in another zoo, or the humiliating claptrap of a circus troupe. The lion appeared to be scared and hostile. And he smelled like a lion.

Most of those who speak of 'lion smell' have never smelled a lion. Because lions don't smell, they stink, they run over the smelling faculty with a permanent acid stench that assaults the lungs of the victim, pumping blood straight to the top of the brain, alerting him explosively to the pestilence. That's how Monaguillo smelt. And this indelible perfume forever impregnated the walls of my apartment, where my wife and I hosted him for two weeks.

I had once seen a film where a blonde and well-built lion tamer nursed a cub in her arms while feeding him milk with a bottle – although judging by the volume of her pectoral reserves she would have been perfectly capable of using a more traditional milk dispenser. My wife was not so daring. It's true the animal wandered around the apartment with no leash and it's also true that his initial and frightened hostility had transformed into dangerously mocking gestures and postures. But we decided we would not emulate the blonde lion-tamer. Maybe because Monaguillo, in spite of his young age, already inspired sincere respect when he showed his fangs or waved his swordlike claws around – even if he only meant it as a game.

After fifteen days and two sofas, destroyed by his mischievous biting, we decided the time had come for Monaguillo to settle in the yard of the Santa Fé house which had been fully kitted out especially for him, with a huge tree to provide him with some shade and everything. I should point out that this house is situated in the heart of a residential neighbourhood of Bogotá. An area of old decaying mansions converted into schools, offices, or refuges for spinsters from good families who watch television, breed canaries, and knit crochet.

This is where Monaguillo was king for over three years. He arrived on a Saturday, amid the incredulity of players and directors who swore never to assign me an impossible mission again. At the beginning he was a free king, enjoying his right to wander around the rooms of the house, bursting footballs with his teeth and scratching his back on the legs of Carlos Pandolfi, an Argentine centre-forward the animal seemed especially fond of. Later, when he grew, he became a captive king: captive in his enormous yard.

The presence of a lion behind the front plants aroused the curiosity of the schoolchildren. Large gangs of intrigued young scholars would form each morning and each afternoon in front of Monaguillo's gate. Mostly the lion snoozed indifferently as they called his name and whistled. But from time to time he would concede the gift of a roar, a rampant gesture or a snort that would have forced the prophet Daniel to take a step back. The schoolchildren would then declare themselves satisfied and, partly scared partly happy, they would move on to occupy themselves with matters more beneficial to their academic future.

It would be redundant to state that every one of them identified emotionally both with the lion and with the club that gave him a home in its shield and flag. In the meantime, Monaguillo travelled to the stadium in a special cage every time Santa Fé played at home and took the pitch together with the team. I remember that, when his weight and his relative harmlessness still allowed it, the one in charge of carrying him and greeting the public with Monaguillo in his arms was Rafael Pacheco, a central defender who visited the lion during the week, spoke to him as if he were a fox terrier and stroked him lengthily behind the ear.

The team looked proud of being identified with the fierceness of the lion. And I am of the impression that Monaguillo was one of the crucial elements which enabled us to win the national championship in that year of 1975. It was the last time to this date.

In time, Monaguillo started developing some worry-ing urban habits that Tarzan never managed to detect in Numa, his regular feline comrade. When he heard exces-sive shouting from the neighbouring house, which had been turned into a primary school, he climbed the tree in three jumps, from there conquered the top of the wall, and walked to and fro menacingly along the dividing wall. The children's panic would shortly be followed by silence. And

Monaguillo, satisfied, would return to his den to continue his siesta.

Thus I learnt a lesson I will not forget if I ever need to travel to Kenya: not only can lions climb trees, they are also capable of executing numerous varieties of balancing acts on a row of bricks. Another lesson I learnt later is that they are also fond of ham and cheese sandwiches. We knew it because the board of directors held meetings in a room on the second floor with a window that overlooked the yard. These often turned into long nocturnal sessions with a lot of sandwiches, a lot of coffee, and a lot of numbers. After a few hours, and while everything else was dark and quiet in the old house, some members of the board would open the windows to freshen the smoke-filled air and while doing so would throw the leftovers to the expectant lion.

Four or five meetings were enough for Monaguillo to develop the conditioned reflex that gave Pavlov – and Independiente Santa Fé – so many headaches. The lion managed to learn that, when the light of the boardroom was switched on, food would be coming his way. And if within ten minutes a piece of bread with ham and cheese had not fallen from the skies, the beast would take to roaring tempestuously to ensure attention was paid to him. Given that all this happened after 10 p.m., the neighbours started to protest and the local municipality accepted their case. We opted for meeting in the dark, but the lion had a foolproof sense of smell. Consequently, and in light of renewed pressure from the authorities, it became necessary to transfer Monaguillo to the zoo nearest to the city.

In his new habitat he knew a lioness in the biblical

sense and reproduced. His children and grandchildren continue to be the official mascots of Santa Fé, although none of them has ever repeated Monaguillo's Sunday trips to the stadium. Of him they spoke and speak still in the press; even a novel by the Argentine writer Roberto Fontanarros devotes many pages to this lion, supporter of the attacking football Santa Fé played in those days.

Monaguillo was killed by an injection from the hands of a clumsy student vet on a certain day I have chosen to forget. He now awaits the resurrection of dead lions as a piece of beautiful reddish leather in the house of 'Chiva' Cortes, the president who made the mistake of believing in Monaguillo and in me.

Death in the stadium

Monaguillo's expulsion from Bogotá's urban radius was one of the hardest moments of my life as football director. But it wasn't the worst. The worst was the death of 'Pulpa' Etchemendi.

'Pulpa' was an excellent Uruguayan coach then serving at Deportivo Cali. I think he was called Washington, like all Uruguayans, or maybe it was Wilson. The truth is that on a Sunday afternoon – I no longer remember if it was in 1976 or 1977 – Santa Fé were playing away against the fearsome Cali, and I went with the team wearing my official delegation hat.

I wish I hadn't gone, because it turned out to be a tragic date. 'Pulpa' fell victim to a treacherous heart attack in the middle of the game, and I have always had the bad idea that I had something to do with that death. Yes, worn down by remorse and anguish, I have to confess that I killed 'Pulpa' Etchemendi. And if I didn't do it alone, I'm afraid I contributed, regrettably, to the sum of the parts which triggered his unfortunate death.

'Pulpa' was a polite bloke and a full-time professional, one of those who spends twenty-four hours a day thinking about the ball, the rival, and how to achieve the ball's penetration of the rival's goal. He had been a very successful manager in Uruguay from where he had been imported by Cali to lead a team of the highest calibre. I had met 'Pulpa' a few months earlier, when he came with Cali to Bogotá, and when we went to his home ground he invited me to sit next to him to watch the youth match which preceded Santa Fé v Cali. One hour before kick-off, we politely said goodbye and each of us headed towards our respective changing room.

From the twenty-sixth minute of the first half, Deportivo Cali were winning 1-0. But with six minutes to go before half time, Recupero, a crafty Argentine midfielder who played for Santa Fé, pinched Calero – the craftiest of the Cali boys – so as to provoke him. Calero responded by kicking Recupero in the stomach. The ref hadn't seen the pinch, but he did see the kick and Calero was sent off.

Soon afterwards, just before the half-time whistle, Bolanos, one of Santa Fé's defenders, suffered a blow to his head and was taken off the pitch on a stretcher.

When I went into the dressing room Bolanos looked like a zombie and the manager didn't know whether he could count on him for the second half or not. The worst thing was that the Santa Fé doctor was sick and hadn't travelled with us, so there was no one to take care of Bolanos. So, armed with my authority as delegate and my concern for Bolanos, I ran across to the Cali dressing room in search of a doctor who could see to him.

As soon as I arrived, I heard the hysterical shouting of 'Pulpa'. He was screaming at Calero for falling for the trap cunningly laid by Recupero. Now they had to face the entire second half with only ten men. He seemed beside himself and was so livid he was having difficulty speaking.

'Pulpa' began choking when he saw a delegate from the enemy camp – that is, myself – standing at the door of his dressing room chatting to his team doctor. He bellowed that there were spies about, went purple, yelled at me to get out, and slammed the changing room door. The doctor and I, ashamed, sneaked back to the place where Oscar Bolanos was swaying into unconsciousness.

Ten minutes later play was resumed. 'Pulpa', not recovered from his congestion, was watching the game from the sideline when the heart attack took place. He was aided by the same doctor who had just advised Bolanos not to return to the field.

That night, while a shaken delegation from Santa Fé attended 'Pulpa's' wake, the doctor told me the coronary had been fatal: when the veteran manager hit the floor, he was already dead. The entire stadium saw him go off on a stretcher, with the game still 1-0, towards a hospital where resuscitation techniques as desperate as they were useless were tried.

'Pulpa' – a good man – would never know that Pepe Tebez scored for Santa Fé with a shot from midfield to draw the match in the seventy-third minute. Nor that those 20,000 spectators before whom he was paraded were convinced, because that was the merciful version offered by the radio, that he had merely fainted.

I also believed that to start with. But when the match

ended and we heard the tragic truth, I was shocked to such an extent that I have been forever convinced that by turning up at the rival's changing room, I killed 'Pulpa' Etchemendi. When I remorsefully left the wake, I knew I had a sensitive heart and, therefore, that I lacked the necessary aptitude to continue being a football director.

Translated by Marcela Mora y Araujo.

saturday night ennui

No doubt about it, Russell was one funky gardener. 'Plant care with attitude' could well have been his maxim. He soon became a good neighbour too. But he was probably the last person in our street I'd have chatted to about football. Krishnamurti or Kerouac perhaps, conspiracy theories definitely, or UFOs if the mood took him. But then you could never tell with Russell.

Shuffling downstairs from my desk, either bored, stiff, or both, I'd see him out there in the garden; tall, thin and greying, with his panama hat and wicker basket, inspecting flowers, primly potting and pruning away like an English gardener from central casting. It was no surprise to learn that he'd once been an actor.

He and I kept a manly sort of distance at first. Being agreeable, agreeing to differ, but what the hell, chatting on, our tea breaks growing ever longer. Gradually the lawn revived. A thousand flowers bloomed. Then Russell stopped charging for his work and spent more time in our kitchen, eating, drinking and confounding our preconceptions. But never a word about football. Not Russell.

Until one afternoon, last June.

Knowing that I was interested – being sort of 'in the business' and all that – he haltingly asked whether, if ever I was watching one of the World Cup games on television and if there was any room on the sofa, could he perhaps come over and watch. He said it wasn't quite the same on his black and white set at home. (Well yes, he admitted, he had once owned a colour television, until, during an episode of *EastEnders*, he counted eleven story lines, every one of them negative. So naturally the TV had to go.)

'But Russell,' I said, 'surely you don't like football.'

And of course he said – because of course you knew that he would say this, or at least something like this – 'Oh no, I dig football. I mean, maybe not as much as cinema or music or gardening, but yeh . . . why, are you so surprised? I mean, do I give off that vibe?'

So the following night Russell and I hunkered down matily in the living room for Holland against Belgium at the Stade de France, and for some reason I came over all self-conscious; not wanting to appear like a testosterone-driven maniac with a baseball bat under my cushion, yet still wanting to show off, just a bit. So I blabbed something or other about how the Stade de France looks great but has lousy toilets, about Jaap Stam having just cost Manchester United several packets, and how the Belgians had a player called Boffin. Russell showed polite interest, but as the game gradually sank into a dull stalemate we turned most of our attention to the curry-filled cartons delivered to the door by a nice young Albanian in a white coat with epaulettes. (Life's like that in our part of London.)

Soon surrounded by spattered plates and shards of poppadom, breathless and bloated by our greed, we slumped back, each trying our best not to fart, while complaining petulantly about all these professional foot-ballers from boring countries being so inept, when neither of us could even be bothered to get up to fetch more beer from the fridge.

Five minutes into the second half, Hasselbaink and Winter, I think it was, forced the Belgian 'keeper to make a couple of smart saves, and us to remember why we were sitting there. Oh yes, the World Cup.

Russell, I realised, was now staring hard at the screen, as if he'd just spotted someone he knew in the Stade de France.

Finally he said, 'I used to be a goalkeeper once.'

I looked over to him and went, 'Oh yeh?'

And like George Fame he said 'Yeh yeh,' and this is what he said.

He said, 'No really, I was about ten at the time . . .'

Sensing another Russell yarn, and feeling too weak to resist, I said, 'Go on then.'

So he did.

'There was this girl called Glynis at our school,' he began. 'Acton Lane primary school it was. She had red hair in ringlets. I'd have done anything to attract her attention. Those ringlets, they drove me wild. Anyway, there was always a bunch of kids playing football in the playground, but never me. I just wasn't interested. But this kid, Raymond Monaghan, he comes up to me one day and says, "You, in goal." '

In the Stade de France, Holland were on the attack. Then they weren't.

'Ray was the school bully,' Russell went on, 'but not a bad bully, if you know what I mean. I was the tallest kid in the class, and he was only short and round-faced, but he just had this way of getting people to do what he wanted. So I went in goal, just for a lark really, but partly hoping that Glynis might be somewhere around watching. Anyway, pretty soon the other team decided they should have a penalty. Well I wasn't sure if Glynis was watching or not but whatever, I managed to save it. Not just stop the ball going in, though. I mean, really save it, diving through the air like a real goalkeeper, like that Belgian guy just then, clutching the ball, pressing it into my body and falling to the ground without making a fool of myself. On tarmac too.'

'Bloody poseur,' I laughed.

'Yeh,' he agreed, 'but I still don't know how I managed it. It was as if I'd suddenly become possessed. As if, just for a fleeting second, I'd sprouted angel wings. I dunno, is there a sporting equivalent of invoking the Muse, or finding the groove? There must be, surely.'

'Wow, Russell,' was all I could manage. But then, I am easily impressed.

So I hit the mute button on the remote, and while in the Stade de France Belgium continued to soak up the Dutch pressure with monotonous efficiency, put on a Deep Forest CD that usually goes well with *Match of the Day* – football as ballet, TV as wallpaper, pygmy chants hanging in the air – and gave myself up to Saturday night ennui.

'And . . .?'

'Well, whatever had possessed me, it felt good,' Russell continued. 'I dunno, maybe that's how all goalkeepers start. They experience that first flight through the air, and a bit like going on a roller coaster, they either hate the experience or want to do it again.'

'Did Glynis see you?'

'No, I don't think so, but by then all the kids were

coming up to congratulate me for saving the penalty, and that was it. Ray Monaghan told me that from now on I was in goal.'

'And . . .'

'I still wasn't too sure, because you have to remember that in those days . . .'

'Which days?'

'I dunno . . . 1954 I suppose. Yeh, I was ten in 1954.'

Nineteen fifty-four? I searched deep into my memory, found in it an old anorak hanging up somewhere, and considered the data. Nineteen fifty-four. That was the year before I was born. Hold on then. Wolves won the League. West Brom beat Preston in the Cup final. Liverpool went down, Everton came up.

A different world.

(Checking these facts later I noticed also that Huddersfield finished third, above Manchester United, and that in the Second Division Doncaster finished above West Ham and Derby.)

Yeh. A different world.

'Anyway, someone must have told Mr Weddle, one of the teachers, and the next thing I know I'm on Stonebridge Rec playing for the school team. I never owned any boots so I suppose someone must have found some for me. I'm pretty sure I never had any kit. No one did in those days. In fact I barely remember any of the teams playing in colours. Just grey or browns, and white.'

At the Stade de France, Dennis Bergkamp trotted on as a substitute for Hasselbaink, looking all sanctimonious, like he does. I was still watching, sort of.

'There was a bombsite just near to the playing fields,' Russell was saying. 'We used to play hide and seek there, or games like Tin Can Tommy, throwing stones at tin cans. A Tuppenny Single for the winner.'

'A what?'

'A Tuppenny Single. A cigarette. You could buy one Weights cigarette for two pence. When England Invaded Germany Hitler's Troops Surrendered. WEIGHTS, you know. Christ, I'm beginning to sound like Tommy Handley. Hey, is that Dennis Bergkamp?'

'Yes it is, and . . .?'

'Yeh, so it turns out we're a pretty good team. Little Ray Monaghan sorted out the opposition, you know, hard man in the middle and all that – he was a fair boxer even then – and there was this nippy kid with knock knees who played on the wing, Davie or Dickie or someone. Wingers were big in those days. I mean, even I'd heard of Stanley Matthews, and I knew bugger all about football.

'And there was me, flying through the air like Lex Christian, the airborne padre in the *Eagle*. I just seemed to have discovered the knack. God knows how, but I just loved that thud, you know that "blat" sound when I caught the ball cleanly.'

I was about to trot out some cliché about how heavy those old lace-up balls were, especially to head, but instead found myself thinking, wouldn't Memory Lane make a great name for an old football ground.

Russell went on. 'Maybe one of the things I liked was the smell of the leather. You were out there on the grass, scooping up the fresh air, away from all the noise and stink of the city, faintly aware of your own sweat and your own pulse, and then suddenly this ball just flies into your hands. And just for a few seconds you could nurse the ball close to your face and breathe in its sort of mustiness. I don't know why I remember that. I haven't thought about this for years. Forty years. More.'

'Do you think,' said Russell after a pause, 'that goalies have a different relationship with the ball?'

'Course they do,' I assured him. 'There's loads of stuff about it. *Goalkeepers Are Different* – one of Brian Glanville's stories. *The Goalkeeper's Fear of the Penalty* – an arthouse film. Er . . . and plenty more, I'm sure of it. It's all well documented.'

'Yeh?' said Russell, almost relieved. 'I can dig that. I mean just look at those guys there on TV. All the outfield players just want to get rid of the ball, use it like a weapon. Bam, bam. But the goalkeeper has to absorb it. Like he really wants to nurse it. Then he gives it a little rub, soothes its wounds, maybe has a few words with it, and then, whoosh, sends it out, back into battle.'

'Well I don't know about . . .'

'And all that bouncing business, that was great. Bouncing the ball up and down in the area, strutting about like that Hungarian goalie at Wembley when they slaughtered England. When would that have been?'

'November '53. They beat us 6-3.'

'Yeh, that would be it. I saw that in the local flicks before a Saturday matinee – you know, the *Crimson Pirate*, starring Burt Lancaster, but first, cock-a-doodle-doo, Pathé News – and there was the Hungarian goalie; slick hair and an all-black kit. Pretty cool for Commies. Compared to him, our players all looked like old men. I mean, all the older kids around Acton and Harlesden were getting into Rock and Roll by then and starting to dress like Bill Haley, and there were Stanley Matthews and Billy Wright dressed like our teachers.'

'And . . .?'

'So I started to become a bit of a hero, I suppose. Saving shots. Shouting out instructions. Trying to hoof this soggy ball as far as I could without breaking my toes. I was like Robert Redford in *The Natural*. You know, when he plays this baseball dude who can't stop scoring home runs, and no one knows how he does it, time after time.'

'Until he meets Kim Basinger.'

'Yeh well, Glynis never did turn up. But by then I didn't care. I'd found something I was good at, and we were beating all these school teams from Willesden and Acton and Ealing and places like that. I still didn't have a clue what all the games were, you know, like Cup games or what. I just turned up and played for myself, hoping our defence would be crap so that I'd have plenty of chances to leap about and show off. I remember once soaring diagonally across the goal, catching the ball and then, as I landed, rolling over a few times. That really seemed to impress the others, so that became part of my repertoire, whether I needed to roll or not. I imagined it was a continental sort of thing to do, like wearing your raincoat over your shoulders or spitting very accurately. Mr Weddle got really pissed off with me for being such a flash little bastard.'

Belgium started to counter-attack. Then they ran out of steam.

Not so Russell.

'One Saturday after we'd played a school game in the morning a few of us went down to a proper match, Brentford maybe, or was it Fulham? Anyway there was this really odd-looking goalkeeper playing for some team from the north. Like a character in an Arthur Askey film, he was; all coal dust, Adam's apple and elbows, but bloody good, or at least he seemed like it to us, because we always thought northerners were better than the London teams. They just looked harder or hungrier, I don't know why. Maybe they were hungrier. Didn't players earn fuck all in those days? Anyway, we're standing right behind the goal, and at the end of the game – I dunno, maybe he'd heard a few of us taking the piss – he comes right up to where we're standing behind the railings and we're thinking, oh shit, he's going to call a copper or something, and instead he . . .'

'Don't tell me, he tossed you his bag of boiled sweeties?'

'Hey, that's right. How did you know?'

'Oh come on, Russ, it was a favourite goalie's trick. Charlie Wright of Grimsby in the sixties, he was famous for it. It was old hat even then.'

For a moment Russell looked dispirited.

'Well maybe it was, but we didn't know what was in the bag until it split open as we were fighting for it, and all these mint humbugs fell out over the terrace. Man, this was like manna from heaven to us, because there was still rationing at that time. So we were like well set up on the walk home, seeing how long we could make the mints last. And meanwhile I was thinking, hey, goalkeepers are like gods, you know. Like a race apart. They wear different gear. They save the day, and they're good guys too. Yeh! And I'm one of them.'

'Russell,' I laughed, 'looking for a role, even then.'

'Oh yeh, and it wasn't just playing. I mean, you know how close Harlesden is to Wembley. My mum and dad had the first television in the street, so every Cup final day we'd have maybe fourteen, fifteen people crammed into our living room. And when a goal was scored, we kids would rush over to the window, stick out our heads, and if the wind was in the right direction you could hear the crowds cheering. Imagine that.'

I imagined it, and heard the distant roar.

'But the best was when England played Scotland at Wembley. As soon as the game was over all the boys in our street would run up to Craven Park, dozens of us, more, standing on garden walls, lining the pavements, waiting for the coachloads of Scottish fans to drive past on their way to having a major piss-up in the West End. It was a real tradition. And then as the coaches went by we'd all shout out at the top of our voices, "Throw out your mouldies! Throw out your mouldies!"'

'Throw out your what?'

'Your mouldies,' repeated Russell. 'I don't know where the word came from, but I'm pretty sure that's what we shouted. Or was it, "Throw out them oldies?" Any rate, the coach windows would open and all these drunk Scots would toss out coins to us boys. Pennies, sixpences, or if they'd won maybe even a half crown or two. We even got a ten bob note once. Can you believe that?'

I couldn't, but Russell absolutely insisted, and anyway, why would he make it up? 'Different world,' he repeated. 'Different world.'

For a moment or two we settled back into our cushions, like wistful old codgers in a home.

Finally, I asked Russell, 'So what about your school team? Did any of the boys go on to become professional players?'

'Not that I know of,' he said slowly. 'I think the centre half, Dougie, played in a pub team when he was a teenager. But we all went off to different schools that summer and so I lost touch with most of them.'

'What about Ray Monaghan?'

'Ray Monaghan,' said Russell, sitting up dramatically, 'became a legend. And I mean, a legend. If I'd been a film director I'd have made a film about Ray Monaghan. When he was seventeen or thereabouts he was driving like crazy around Harlesden one afternoon when he had a smash. One of the other guys in the car, John Wilson, said Ray was crushed by the steering wheel, but he was that hard that he staggered out of the wreckage, covered in blood, teeth and all smashed, went round to the front of the car and started punching the mangled bonnet and going "You fucking bastard" to the car. "You fucking bastard. You fucking bastard." Three times, just like that, people walking by, watching in amazement. And then he just collapsed and died on the road. A boxer to the end. Someone should have put that in a film.'

As Russell was recounting this Patrick Kluivert must have been having similar memories, because the next thing we saw he was giving one of the Belgians some lip and suddenly his elbow was up. The Belgian went down, and out came the red card. Sure to God it's a tough old world out there. Poor Ray Monaghan. And then I remembered that Kluivert had been in trouble over a car crash. Or was that another Dutchman? Christ, I'd eaten a lot of curry.

'So what happened to your goalkeeping?'

Russell's eyes screwed up as he followed Kluivert's anguished departure. I wondered if the question was a painful one. Had something awful happened, like an accident on the pitch, or him having to give up football in order to tend his dying mother. Or maybe Glynis swanned off with one of the other players.

'Russell!' I repeated. 'What happened?'

'What?'

'What happened to your goalkeeping?'

'Oh that? I stopped all that.'

'Stopped? Why? Were you injured? What happened?'

Russell paused further. For dramatic effect, perhaps, or because he'd not thought about it for years. Or maybe he'd just had enough of football for one night.

Eventually he looked up, engaged my eyes in that steely way of his, and said, 'I just lost it.'

'What do you mean, lost it?'

'I mean just that. I lost it. Whatever "it" was. The magic. The gift. The fearlessness. My angel's wings had been clipped.'

'Just like that? When, how?'

'Oh I dunno, I think we were having a kickabout on Stonebridge Rec, kids from the school, local kids. It was after the winter, but the pitch was like a mud-heap, and I was cold, and my hands were all caked in it, and this kid, Siddiqui Senior he was called, one of the few Asian kids in our area – a big guy, maybe a foot taller than me, a few years older, much bigger than I'd ever had to face before, so this was like "the real thing" – and he was just coming at me with the ball, coming at me, with all the other kids screaming for me to get him, even though I was scared shitless. But I went out to him, and as he got closer and closer I had to go down in the mud.

'I went down. He went down. And we just sort of crashed into each other. Whack! Knees, shins, elbows, the lot. And as I lay there, face down, nose poking in the wet, smelling the mud, breathing hard, I just said to myself, "Fuck it". Just like that. Fuck it.'

For a while the two of us sat silently, watching Holland and Belgium play out the dying embers of their goalless draw on TV.

And then Russell went home, and we never talked about football again. Only gardening, and life.

Oh yes, always life.

at the beginning is the ball

JORGE VALDANO

'Air with a leather lining'
Wenceslao Fernandez Flores

. . . Periphery, sacrifice, hopelessness. Neighbourhood and misery. Only the ball produces a stimulus pleasant enough to forget that shit life. They express their talent playing football because football is the only thing they have left, the only thing that makes them happy and free. They run, they jump, they fight. They lock two bare feet and sparks fly because nothing is more serious for them at that moment which belongs entirely to them and in which they have compromised even their soul . . .

At the beginning is the ball, world at their feet, first love and I'm not exaggerating. At night they hug it to go to sleep, while they eat they stroke it with their sole under the table; later, with time, they look for the space to play. The ball helped me to be a child, but it's also still rolling around serious memories. I was four years old on a cloudy day when they took me to hospital so that an unforgettable butcher could keep my tonsils. Back home I went out to the backyard to seek comfort with the ball, but my mother, with the shout of 'today's not a day to play football', sent me back to bed. And I was five years old when a scandalised aunt pulled me out of a street match on another one of those days that wasn't a day to play football and returned me to my father's funeral. This article has no biographical intentions but I find no better way to describe how real life became when they took the ball away from me.

The ball. Fascinating toy that populates our childhood with unusual friends and foes: a wall can be a good team-mate, a chair a serious rival. To make the ball obedient, to understand its effects, to make our speeds agree, that's what the game consists of. The ball invites us to follow it, to broaden our possibilities, to create original movements. I tend to think the game begins in the head (understanding the game), but I must admit that the learning process necessarily starts with the feet (under-standing the ball). It's impossible to play football if the ball is another adversary. Recently, during a visit to my home town, I peeked into the eternal vacant lot and heard the eternal wise guy take pity on the eternal clumsy one: 'Hey, ball, leave that poor boy alone!' There was the childhood, which I had left behind long ago, keeping its sacred code: in Argentina it means a lot, in a bad sense, to not be good at playing football.

I need to make it clear, so as not to put my memory to more discomfort, that to me the ball is 'la pelota'. I believe it is important to see it as feminine, such a crucial love.

As we all know, football is prior even to itself; in fact there is no civilisation, however old, that doesn't believe it laid the first stone of this game. Running in a disorderly manner after a spherical form is part of an ancient need for mockery and derision. It was in England that football branched out from rugby, found its geographical frontiers and started to establish a set of simple and wise rules.

Until it found its popular personality the game was aristocratic (due to its passage through exclusive schools) and proletariat (it filled the idle hours of the first sons of industrialisation). The people had access to a salary, to some free time, and to participate in the entertainments of the rich. Football got divided into spectators and practitioners, which meant that as massive societies were born the stadium became the first symbol of social integration.

The Empire sent its ships out to trade throughout the world and in the itinerary they sowed football. In some suitcases, a ball travelled; in many ports, a match was played; in almost every country British sailors and workers started to transmit a passion which grew effortlessly . . . Already a ball was bouncing in the Rio de la Plata.

Then come the people

> 'Football is a sunny afternoon, the ball bouncing, the shout of a goal ending in an embrace. Football is nice, clean and transparent.'
> Eduardo Rafael

My memory is plural because it is very similar to the memory of any South American football player; in fact, the individualism, vice of which we are accused, is only the desire to keep the ball in our power that little bit longer, a possessive desire that starts with that first relationship. That's how we grow up, in love with something that propositions us to enjoy, to create and to dream.

The memory advances: I hear the shouts and see the disorder of a small army, in an empty lot, running after the ball. Our only compromise was with freedom but without knowing it we were learning to live. We still played ball more than football. There were two teams and two goals, but we were seeking individual exhibitions before collective efficiency – a very Argentine trait and not only in football. Enemies are obstacles which are necessary so that we can learn to pass them, tease them, for us to show off. Friends are disturbing because they ask for the ball. It's considered an interference to such an extent that, Angel Cappa reminds me, in Argentina the way we shout for the ball has for decades been 'take it' rather than 'touch it'. Understand this clearly: someone in my team has the ball and I, wanting it, shout at him: 'take it'; that is, before I receive it I am promising an urgent return so he will make me a partner of his move. If he gives it to me, the normal thing is that I will not keep my promise and that's why he, who's known this for genera- tions, doesn't pass it to me.

The ball runs, jumps, flies, and with her as an excuse the delicate system of child communication gradually gets adjusted. Sometimes children try to be adults and don't succeed, like in those fancy dress parties where at the beginning everyone seems to be what they're pretending but at the end of the afternoon the clown's make-up is smeared and he's bored, the cowboy's lost his gun and cries in the corner, and the ballet dancer has lost her *joie de vivre* ever since she wet her pants. Footballers' projects always jump to imaginary stadiums like little lead soldiers, but formality bursts at the start of each game. Pleasure versus obligation, desire versus responsibility, freedom versus order. Who wins? The ball, bouncing between a cloud of dust and a swarm of children who soon forget their intent of manhood.

Football arrived everywhere in a similar way, but in each country it found a different mould, as if the miracle of identification adhered to the sensibility of each land. The beach, the heat, and the black influence gave football a hop of joy in Brazil. Argentina had different migratory currents and the climate is different, therefore football's rhythm has a different breath. Two defined styles with some points in common: football as a feeling, the prestige which starts with ball control and a high degree of competitiveness.

A new people disembark and find in football a good excuse for integration. Spanish, Italians, Germans, Englishmen and *Criollos* formed, in the suburbs, swarms running after the ball. The joy was liberating and made one forget the sacrifice of the immigrants, who had begun to understand that 'making America' was much harder than they had dreamed. People gathered to watch those madmen and their display of courage and ability. Around the ball the country started to get together, the entire continent because, in South America more than anywhere else in the world, football is the people . . .

'A childhood orphaned of toys will always have the consolation of a ball'
Enrique Gonzalez Tuñon

All the sentimental truths about the vacant lot cannot make us neglect the essential character: the owner of the ball. Pedagogic kid who teaches, from the start, where real power lies; son of a banker, fat little rich kid who is always late to state clearly how important he is. Disastrous footballer and always makes the first team, you'll understand. A very important guy, but only until the match starts. From that moment on the best is in command: a cheeky smartass with no shoes. The prestige of the skilful! He is envied because everyone wants the ball but the ball only wants him, the skilful one, the fucking big head and rightly so. He has moral command over the group, a democratic street election which, almost always, votes for the scummy low life because it is there, in the misery, where great football is cultivated. It's comforting to think that there are still kingdoms for the dispossessed, even if they're not serious ones.

One ball is enough for all, and if there's a space, all you need then is enthusiasm. The ages can mix together. Ten-year-old kids play with twelve-year-old veterans, who, in turn, have acquired some wisdom playing next to blokes who have made it to the unreachable age of fourteen. That's how football, one of the more authentic cultural expressions, transmits its message from generation to generation. If culture, as Mao said, 'is the memory of a people', why not apply this concept to this popular phenomenon that beats time and progress each and every time? When you play, you learn to be a certain way, a set of national vices and virtues which when I was a kid we called 'ours'. Common obsessions, a voice of our own which is not better than anyone's but sounds different to every other one. That's the source, that's where general notions about 'our' style come from, and we establish agreements based around arguable neighbourhood laws which are nevertheless unshiftable: cheekiness is prestigious, delays are unforgivable, and running too much is a defect, to cite but three examples.

Time and sensitivities can pervert such raw material but I think, like Borocoto (unforgettable journalist), that 'one must always keep, in some twist of the ear, a little dust from the vacant lot'.

. . . All the people? Yes, no one's left out but, as is always the case, while the poor play the rich guide and decide from outside. People on the pitch, people on the terraces, people in the suburbs where football is the rival of school. Its teachings are not academic, on the contrary, talent is exercised on the difficulty of an uneven terrain and in enthusiastic disorder. The best will end up fascinating an audience that was always sensitive to the magic of the virtuous. They say that Ricardo Bochini, a player for Independiente in the 1970s and 1980s but an idol forever, was called up to play for Argentina in a friendly. In the first half he served no less than five passes which were wasted by his team-mates in an undignified way. At half-time, Cesar Luis Menotti, then coach, came up to him to tell him to go on playing well and not to worry. Bochini replied with a thread of a voice: 'If we carry on like this I'm going to have to score the goals myself.' Don't even think of it, master. The goal is to be scored or missed by another, you are an artist who should not stoop to practical tasks. Bochini's story is similar to Argentine football and to my own childhood, which is why I mention it here as a symbol of a football flame which is going out . . .

The end of childhood

'As well as its own beginning, the beginning of the bounce and of independence, the team provides the ball with the engine of eleven malices and eleven imaginations.'
Jean Giraudoux

Still with much dust inside the ear someone starts to impose limits on the uncontrollable desire to play. It's usually an older guy who will spoil, with love and forever, the disorderly freedom of those improvised games. He builds a team with the best from the neighbourhood, gives them all a uniform shirt and sets an objective: to beat the guys from the other neighbourhood.

When a referee appears, with a whistle, a watch, and all that, we suspect the joke is over. The stomach is weighed down by something similar to excitement, but also to fear. It's a matter of defending a territory, or, put another way, of defending the pride of a community. It is the time to show off ability, with its jesting prestige, but also courage, or else they could think ... That's the moment where football is discovered as a union matter. Up to here, one felt like the belly button of the world and the ball was the belly button of football but now the other begins to exist and the ball socialises her behaviour allowing us to discover the game as a cooperative effort. It doesn't mean that it has to be less fun just because collective responsibilities arrive bringing with them collective obligations. After all, there is some pleasure in giving, some satisfaction in receiving.

The truth is that one shouts 'touch it' and another 'come back' and another 'open up' and another one goes and says 'mark that guy and stop staring at the ball like a moron' which is like saying 'forget the vacant lot, this is a pitch for real'. Each one starts to understand what he's good for, which is the position that suits him best, but sometimes someone rebels and at the fourth touch he realises that at least three were too many and not because he loses the ball, which he does, but because half the team is bringing him back to reality: 'Let her go, you're not playing alone, you fucking wanker.' That's when you finally understand, forever and painfully, that the ball belongs to everyone. The time has come to become a man.

The great ideas have stumbled in the world, but in our continent Maradona and Pelé existed. Because there are no longer any social phenomena capable of defending the pride of belonging, football's influence increased; it's a little island where, through bizarre processes of identification, Uruguayans, Brazilians and Argentinians can feel we are somebody. Those crazy English returned, this time without a ball, and they invaded the Malvinas, but football was never in danger because South America has incorporated it as its own. It's not for nothing that they say 'if England is the mother of football, you'll find the father in the Rio de la Plata' – it is well known that the football world welcomes a little vulgarity. And meanwhile, South American footballers are recognised for their ability, personality and tactical culture, to such an extent that they have a presence in every country where football has a commercial presence. There are at least two leagues of wandering South American players going round the world (eight hundred players, maybe a thousand?). For those professionals football is not a game. In the meantime, in the miserable suburbs of any old city, dozens of kids run after a ball as if they were Ronaldo, Maradona, Pelé, Di Stefano... Far away from their dreams, a multitude shouts.

Translated by Marcela Mora y Araujo.

a glittering star in the sky

EAMONN SWEENEY

Sean South of Garryowen was a favourite in the pre-match sing-songs of Jack Charlton's Irish team. A stirring rebel-rouser, the ballad tells the tale of a singularly unsuccessful raid on an RUC barracks during the similarly ill-fated IRA border campaign of the late fifties.

> 'Twas on a dreary New Year's Eve,
> As the shades of night came down,
> A lorry load of volunteers
> Approached the border town.
> There were men from Dublin and from Cork
> Fermanagh and Tyrone
> But the leader was a Limerick man
> Sean South from Garryowen

The eponymous South bit the dust during the raid, the victim of a decision to carry out a frontal attack which seems to have been made in the belief that a more stealthy approach would not have quite been the sporting thing to do. He became a Republican legend and, although the border campaign, which ran from 1956 to 1962, eventually fizzled out, many of the leaders of the IRA in the Troubles saw their first action there.

It's doubtful if many of the members of the Irish team

singing the song on their way to the Olympic Stadium in Rome knew much about Sean South and his unfortunate demise. He, of course, was never to know that his name would serve as a rallying cry for a team earning their living in a country to which the men who shot him pledged their allegiance. It seems a fair bet that he would not have been too happy about this. Brendan O'Heithir, one of Ireland's finest writers on sport, told of meeting South outside a soccer match in Limerick. South was jotting down the names of those emerging from the ground. He explained to O'Heithir that he was carrying out his duty as a member of a Vigilance Committee, one of the nearest equivalents sport has had to a Stasi.

The Vigilance Committee was perhaps the most malignant growth resulting from The Ban, a rule which for many years forbade members of the Gaelic Athletic Association, Ireland's largest sporting organisation, to play soccer or rugby on pain of expulsion from the association. Attendance at what the GAA called 'Foreign games' could also result in banishment from the ranks. The Vigilance Committees were set up to check just which Association members attended these matches. They could also be found at dances organised by soccer or rugby clubs, events which were also out of bounds to GAA members. The GAA's sports of gaelic football and hurling may have been far more popular than rugby or soccer but, in the spirit of the American blockade of Cuba, they were taking no chances all the same.

The ban was eventually abolished in 1971 when the GAA suffered an uncharacteristic fit of liberalism which may or may not have been occasioned by the memory of Brazil's brilliance in Mexico the year before. But it would be wrong to presume that the mentality which both gave birth to it and prosecuted it with such Salem-like fierceness has disappeared. To paraphrase that latter-day Sean South, Gerry Adams, 'It hasn't gone away, you know.' In the aftermath of the Omagh bombing, a fund-raising soccer match between an Irish selection and a major English League club was planned for the town. The only local ground big enough to hold the anticipated crowd was the GAA ground which was offered to the organisers by the local club only for GAA HQ to put their foot down. The rule which forbids the playing of foreign games in GAA grounds meant that the game could not be played. The fact that American football, Australian Rules and (most unforgivable of all) the music of Simple Minds have all been witnessed at Association venues did not alter their reasoning. Neither did the suggestion that the human tragedy of Omagh should have been enough to cause the suspension of any bureaucracy.

Soccer in Ireland is in a pretty unique position. It's hard to think of anywhere else in the world where the mere playing of the game has been decried by others as an anti-national act of treachery. Add in the fact that just a hundred miles across the sea is the mighty Premier League, hoovering up both emotional and financial support from Ireland as well as the best players in the country, and it's clear that the League of Ireland is caught between two forces which between them make Scylla and Charybdis look pretty inviting options.

The League struggles on under ever-increasing pressure. The pervading influence of Sky has forced the abandonment of the traditional Sunday afternoon kick-off while it has also increased the lure of the all-powerful

English game for young fans who find the reality of a League game something of a comedown after the multi-camera, multi-replay, multi-statistic world of Super Sunday. The talk of Wimbledon moving to Dublin to mop up what support remained there confirmed the most open secret in Irish sport: no one cares what happens to the League of Ireland.

Well, almost no one. I am a follower of the League of Ireland, a position analogous to being an adherent of a minority religion which, like Bahai, Lutheranism or Seventh Day Adventism, is big enough for survival but far too small to really thrive. Like many another follower of an obscure creed, I did not select it, it was passed on to me by my parents and I had been fully initiated before I was old enough to make up my own mind. The same, of course, could be said of Catholicism, which I have managed to shake off, so my support of Sligo Rovers and the League in general is probably not completely pre-determined.

I attended my first Rovers match three days before I was born. My mother and father watched another defeat for The Bit O' Red on the Sunday, I arrived on the Wednesday, some amniotic memory probably informing me that a mile away from the hospital lay a grim ground where I was destined to spend most of my youth and what is either adulthood or a less physically fit continuation of the same youth.

If my mother carried me to my pre-natal debut fixture, it was probably my father's fault that we were there. My father, to put it bluntly, was the kind of person who supported League of Ireland. Born in the working-class terraces of Kilkenny, he had moved to Sligo and followed the game that made most sense to him. The League of Ireland has always been the preserve of the working class, of people from council houses in a country where not owning something meant you yourself were nothing. Its roots further accounted for soccer's strange invisibility in an Ireland whose self-image was rural, a country where the self-sufficient small farmer was the heroic equivalent to a record-breaking tractor-driver on a Soviet poster. There was at least some lip-service paid to the people of Dublin, but town dwellers outside the capital are a strange absence from Irish literature. Soccer was their game.

The concentration of soccer in these towns has always been the subject of adverse comment from those who hold The Ban in their hearts. It is derided as a 'Garrison Game' introduced by British soldiers and there are mutterings about the non-patriotic impulses of the 'Garrison towns' which even broach the subject of miscegenation between the Army and the populace. None of this stuff is particularly pleasant. Let's face it, the British also introduced soccer to Brazil where the locals seem to have no hang-ups about not playing a non-indigenous game, and the small-town estates where soccer is played in Ireland are the same as its heart-lands the world over.

There are a couple of bizarre sidelights to this attack on soccer as a game which is British and therefore suspect, notwithstanding the fact that it does appear to be played in quite a few countries which are not exactly under the Saxon yoke. One is that there is a tendency towards Republican rhetoric from the wilder sections of League of Ireland support and that the depressed areas from which the teams draw this support are often represented at local level by Sinn Fein councillors. Another is that rugby, up to recently at least, was often genuinely the game of the upper classes in small towns but never attracted the same sort of enmity from the GAA. And one final quote from a GAA activist in the sixties calling for the retention of The Ban sums up the temperate and intellectual nature of the debate. Wolfe Tone, said our hero, had died so The Ban would not be removed. Wolfe Tone did indeed die. In 1798, eighty-six years before the GAA was founded.

The status of League of Ireland soccer as the game of the marginalised is underlined by just what has happened since the advent of the newly prosperous Celtic Tiger economy. In a word, nothing. The growth of an affluent middle class has seen the GAA finally embrace corporate culture with the fervour of Native Americans making the acquaintance of whiskey and it has greatly helped the new professional rugby clubs. But the Celtic Tiger, if anything, has been bad for the League of Ireland. It is members of the newly confident business community who are behind the bid to bring Wimbledon to Dublin. In a country where the present day is seen as something of a golden age and the words 'modernity' and 'progress' have totemic significance and almost sacred resonance, the League of Ireland seems too closely connected with an Ireland of the past. A Premiership team based in Dublin would be yet another proof for the lords of the new church that we have indeed come a long way.

Being born in 1968 has made me one of the chosen people in Rovers history. I have witnessed unparalleled success, undreamt of by those who came before me, a whopping three major trophies in thirty years, with the 1977 league followed by the 1983 cup (starring Colin

Oakley ex-Sheffield United, Andy Elliot ex-Manchester City and Gus Gilligan ex-Witney Town) and 1994 cup (featuring Mark McLean ex-Glasgow Celtic, Will Hastie ex-Kilmarnock and Richardo Gabbiadini, on loan from Frickley Athletic).

Rovers' greatest moments have had an American economy style dependence on imported labour. And it doesn't require the toting of an overly tuned pathos detector to wonder about the effect of arriving at The Showgrounds, for many years Spartan enough to make the most homesick veteran of the Battle of Thermopylae feel warmly nostalgic, on players who have spent their apprenticeships, and sometimes more than that, at clubs from a different football planet (Willie McStay, ex-Glasgow Celtic, '94 player-manager; Lawrie Sanchez, ex-Wimbledon, '95 player-manager; Nicky Reid, ex-Manchester City, current player-manager).

There is a certain degree of local pride, tinged with *Schadenfreude*, about the effect a first sighting of The Showgrounds must have had on some of our new arrivals which is why the story of Johnny Cooke, ex-Manchester United, arriving at the ground in the late sixties, is such a favourite. Cooke amazed the club officials by repeating how impressed he was on his first visit to the ground.

The stand?

Super.

The dressing rooms?

Marvellous.

The pitch?

Brilliant. The training facilities are great, I can't wait to see the ground.

The Last Emperor-style downturn in fortunes can

have a bad effect on some people. A visibly disgruntled Lawrie Sanchez seemed to spend most of his time at the club trying to repeat his famous FA Cup final winning header against Liverpool. Free-kick after free-kick, corner after corner, long throw after long throw were directed towards Lawrie who stood at the near post as if trying to recapture the greatest moment of his past like Norma Desmond watching her old videos in her decaying mansion. He was not any more successful than the star of *Sunset Boulevard*, although he did get to say, 'I'm ready for my close-up Mr Hammam,' and we fondly watch him prowl the touch-line in his role as assistant to Joe Kinnear during the unfairly rare Dons television appearances.

If the League of Ireland's proximity to the Football League has ensured and probably will always ensure that Irish domestic soccer remains on a par with that of Malta, Cyprus, Kazakhstan and Albania, it also means that, from time to time, certain stars will, like Jeff Daniels in *The Purple Rose of Cairo*, leave the screen and walk into our reality. They might not quite be the stars they were but they still give the League that exotic flavour of being a cross between Valhalla and the Betty Ford Clinic. A World XI culled from the players who have passed, albeit briefly, through the League would give anyone's selection plenty of it.

A one-eyed Gordon Banks played for St Patricks Athletic against Shams in 1977 and saved around him as Pats won 1-0. Uwe Seeler inexplicably turned up to play one game for Cork Hibs and hit a hat-trick. And George Best, struggling to keep his demons under control, hung around to play a dozen games for Cork Celtic when, before his thirtieth birthday, he should have been the greatest player in the world. The huge crowds came to worship and left in mourning. Peter Lorimer, looking several stone overweight, turned out for UCD in midfield and could hardly get out of the centre-circle. He soon disappeared though not as quickly as a thirty-nine-year-old Steve Archibald who played one half for Dundalk before being sucked into the vortex of the fading athlete. Terry McDermott's time at Cork City was terribly unhappy but his fellow evangelist of the bubble-perm Alan Sunderland helped Derry City into an FAI Cup final. All of them, good or bad, looked out of place without a television to frame themselves.

The League of Ireland is probably, in football terms, a Third World League and as such it has suffered from the trading patterns familiar between First and Third World countries, its valuable resources being stripped away and brought elsewhere for a nominal fee. Once abroad they appreciate massively. I saw Roy Keane as a teenager with Cobh Ramblers and anyone who tells you they could see his potential then is lying. If they say the same about Paul McGrath, they're probably telling the truth but they saw him first as a centre-forward with an afro Antonio Fargas would have disdained as OTT. I saw Ronnie Whelan as a brilliant sixteen-year-old winger with Home Farm and Jim Beglin at Shamrock Rovers looking like the best full-back the league ever had. On the other side of the coin, I saw Johnny Giles finishing his career at Shamrock Rovers, thirty-eight years old, moving at half-pace and not hitting one pass even an inch astray over ninety minutes. I'm glad I saw all of them when they didn't have the television set around them, it somehow makes them more real now.

The amount of Irish players who are signed up by English clubs is phenomenal given the size of the country. So many players are taken out of the country when still in their teens that the League of Ireland is left with a vastly diminished talent pool. And if a Keane or a McGrath does slip through for a couple of years, he will be quickly nabbed once he shows what he's really made of. The scouting system English clubs have over here operates with a Mountie-like efficiency. You never know when the man you've met in the pub across the road from the ground is going to whip out a laminated card which says he's an official Irish scout for Gillingham. Or Huddersfield Town. Or Peterborough. I recently visited a secondary school in Clifden, out in the wild extremities of Connemara in a place where soccer has hardly taken hold at all, and found out that one of the lads I was talking to had been on trial with Derby County. The most run-of-the-mill Sunday League teams seem able to boast a player who has got at least one free flight out of a Premiership side.

This all-seeing scouting system does not really have an equivalent in the League of Ireland. In fact, notwithstanding Uwe Seeler's strange Cork odyssey, the experience of clubs here with foreign players has been disastrous to the extent you would expect, given that few of the putative stars have actually been seen before they arrive in the country. Remember the uproar when it emerged Aston Villa had signed Savo Milosevic purely on video evidence? Even video evidence would have been an unimaginable luxury to a League of Ireland club. Take, for example, the case of Sligo Rovers and Gabriel Ojo.

Sligo, like many another Irish county, is proud of its

Catholic Missionary tradition. One exemplar of this tradition was a football-mad priest who while ministering in West Africa came across a group of local youngsters having a kickabout. Noticing that one of them possessed an extraordinary level of skill, he decided there and then to bring the lad back to Sligo where he could make his name with Rovers.

Gabriel Ojo made his name all right. He is a legend in Sligo, renowned for being the worst footballer ever to play with the club.

The most charitable explanation of what happened was that the priest brought the wrong player. Because poor Ojo was not just bad, he gave the impression of never having kicked a ball before. And his lack of talent was made even more noticeable by his utter incongruity. Even today, Ireland is a pretty homogeneously white country, but in the grim times of 1965 Ojo was extraordinarily exotic. The fact that he played through a bitter League of Ireland winter with no boots on probably did not help him much. So rarely did black people figure in the popular Irish consciousness at the time that Ojo was nicknamed after a South American saint who was a popular staple of the religious magazines on the day. The cry of 'Give to Blessed Martin De Porres on the wing' followed him around for the season. He himself was to be followed by Albanians, Americans, Dutchmen and South Africans, who did not fare much better. As the years went on, their nicknames would be inspired by television rather than religion.

But, paradoxically, if the club have not had the best of luck with foreign players, the most loved figure in the history of Rovers came from furthest away of all. Johnny

Chadda was born in the Punjab and was a member of the Congress Party, he even knew Nehru, during the Indian struggle for independence. In the late forties he decided to make his way to England but could not find enough work in Liverpool to support his family. Someone told him that Ireland might be a better bet, an incurable optimist obviously, and he made his way to Sligo where he at first eked out a living as a door-to-door salesman. He had become interested in football while in college in India and offered his services to the struggling club. In the past forty years he has been President, Chairman, Treasurer, Secretary and general non-executive dogsbody for Rovers. He also became a teacher, learning the Irish language in a month to pass his interview in the local diocesan college. Johnny's most famous moment, I think, sums up why people continue to follow teams like Sligo Rovers.

Because, if you think about it, it is little short of miraculous that the League of Ireland keeps going at all. Next door to the most hyped league in the world and assailed by televised soccer on every side, it is made up of the kind of clubs who have no place in a future where only the giants will matter. It will be difficult enough for Crystal Palace and Coventry City in that future; Sligo Rovers, Bohemians and Limerick City will be facing the equivalent of a Nuclear Winter. Yet I do not think the league will die. League of Ireland people gritted their teeth against the onslaught of The Ban and kept their teams going, and they will do the same thing against Murdoch. Rovers is one of the only football clubs, maybe the only one, in the world run as a Co-Operative Society. It keeps going because people like myself pay in a few quid every month as if we were part of the footballing equivalent of a Christmas Club, knowing that what we'll get at the end won't be great but that if we don't put up the cash we'll get nothing at all. We are fiercely determined to resist the Dirty Digger's attempts to buy the club. I mean, we've got to be next in line.

Anyway what hope has Murdoch got against Johnny Chadda who in 1994, after we had won the Cup for the second time, shoved his way through the crowds at Sligo Town Hall, got in front of the civic dignitaries and recited, in the accent of the Punjab, a poem specially composed for the occasion.

> Even if the sun should stop to shine,
> Even if the wind would stop to blow,
> The name of Sligo Rovers will shine and shine,
> Forever like a glittering star in the sky.

You can't ban that.

a fanfare to the new man: rereading *fever pitch*

LYNNE TRUSS

One day in 1991, I was travelling as a passenger in my boyfriend's car through central London, when road rage erupted. Its suddenness was rather alarming. Traffic around Trafalgar Square was as tight as ever; in our battered Fiesta, we had stopped at the Whitehall lights; and just as we drove forward, a smart little Renault overtook us at speed. At which point, his honour insulted in some obscure way, my boyfriend set off in high dudgeon to race against the Renault. I remember very well my feelings on this occasion, especially when, as the boyfriend made an insane attempt to overtake the Renault on the inside, he clipped it. 'Shit,' he breathed. Both cars slowed, and pulled over; and from the other emerged a young black couple. The man, who had been driving, started to yell.

'Sorry,' my boyfriend said at once – an expression of contrition which was doubly surprising to me, since a) I knew he wasn't sorry in the slightest, and b) it was a word he staunchly avoided at home. However, it certainly came in handy now. 'Sorry,' he said again. 'Sorry, sorry, sorry, sorry, sorry.'

'Are you ****ing *mad*?' the man said, jumping up and down with rage. He swore a lot, and waved his arms.

'Sorry, sorry, sorry,' the boyfriend repeated in a whisper, like a kind of prayer.

The man vented more anger; examined the bumper of the car; and yelled at us again. Naturally, I had quite mixed feelings about this, since I was completely on his side.

But then something astonishing happened; something which places this incident, I believe, very firmly in the early 1990s.

'Oh shit,' he said at last, with a sigh. 'If the women had been driving, this wouldn't have happened, would it? It's our stupid unreconstructed male pride that makes us behave this way.'

As he came towards us to shake hands and practise fashionable male bonding with my idiot boyfriend, I blinked and swallowed, and the word 'Sorry?' came to my own lips at last. I mean to say. *What?* Would you believe it? 'Hit him!' I wanted to say. 'Go on!' Good grief, of all the people in London my boyfriend could collide with, he had collided with a bloody New Man.

Watching men beat themselves up about being men was one of the more entertaining sideshows of the early 1990s. Sometimes I get all wistful for those days that are gone by. Not that I actually liked or trusted many New Men. For one thing, I felt aggrieved to see breast-beating hijacked by people who didn't have breasts. But mainly, I entertained a niggling suspicion that the New Man's public proclamation of his intrinsic unworthiness would inevitably turn out brilliantly to his advantage in the end. 'Oh, this damned testosterone, Milud,' men could say, eventually, in court. 'If it had been women doing that armed robbery, they would never have fired the sawn-off shotguns, would they?' Good grief, no sooner had these chaps discovered what a parcel of emotional cripples they were, than they were actually asking everyone to feel sorry for them.

It was in this context, of course, that Nick Hornby's *Fever Pitch* (1992) was written, published, and first sold in phenomenal quantities. You wondered where all this was leading, and here it is. Yes, *Fever Pitch* may have been the best football book ever written (as it says on the paperback), but if one reads it again in 1999, what one finds above all in this archetypal New Man outpouring is not so much an apology for football as a self-portrait of a damn nice re-educated bloke parading an infantile addiction, and daring us to love him for it. *Fever Pitch* is still a clever, well-written and very charming book, but to re-read it wizened by a few more years of sexual politics is chastening. Were we really taken in by such disingenuous wheedling just a handful of years ago?

Of course, the book's huge success can be placed in other contexts, too. Famously, Hornby introduced football to people who bought books, and books to people who love football, at a time when such a brokering between the two cultures was apparently the last thing required by either. It was a stroke of genius. The Hillsborough disaster of 1989 (and subsequent Taylor Report) had forced the issue of football attendance into the forefront of the news; meanwhile the dizzying excitement of the 1990 World Cup in Italy had raised the profile of English football for the general public. Neither event, however, would have propelled new punters through the turnstiles, and the general perception of the football match (not helped by Bill Buford's *Among the Thugs*) remained as a battlefield for the underclass. Against such a background, it was surprising that a nice, unaggressive Cambridge literature graduate with a self-deprecatory streak and a keen grasp of contemporary gender issues was obsessed by Arsenal Football Club.

Cleverly, Hornby did not apologise for anybody except himself, which was why the book worked. Nowadays we have adverts about men being 'in love' with football teams; the concept of Manchester United ruining one's life is commonplace. But Hornby started all that. Although he famously states that sexual analogies to football never quite work (sex takes place in the warm, for a start), what his book describes essentially is a hapless, punishing, one-way affair with Arsenal. No one had written about the masochism of football support in this way before; they would above all have been embarrassed, conscious of the many more important things in the world. But then along came Nick Hornby, New Man, and started quite a few sentences with 'It embarrasses me to confess', and overnight a lot of these people found that here was a clever, likeable writer who was prepared to analyse exactly what it was like to be them.

I met Nick Hornby last year, when his novel *About a Boy* was published. *The Times* organised a reading with Dillons at London University's Institute of Education, and I interviewed him on stage before taking questions from his fans. He was generous and funny and rather bald, as you might expect. He wore a plain white tee-shirt and had a *Guardian* in a carrier bag. I introduced him by saying that whenever I write fiction, I have one question always in mind, perhaps because I was once told it was the essence of story. 'What do the characters want?' I ask myself.

'Readers must understand the motivation of the characters at all times, so what do these characters want?' The
reason I mentioned this theory was that Nick's books
blithely belie this rule. His characters have no idea what
they want. Wanting things sounds too tiring. He sells
zillions of copies, yet there is no oomph whatsoever in his
books. The protagonist of *About a Boy* is a happy layabout.
In *High Fidelity*, events just happen, without any strenuous
human agency. Even in *Fever Pitch*, Nick's relationship
with Arsenal is more about endurance than impetus. The
conclusion to this comparison was obvious, and a little
hard to take. Fictionally speaking, I'd been barking up the
wrong tree for years.

But this is another reason for *Fever Pitch*'s success, I
would say. In the nicest sense, it's a very unchallenging
book. What it offers, on the contrary, is absolution. Like
his other books, it teaches us that it's OK to be shallow, to
have no ambition, and to lack any kind of broader per-
spective. Hornby is so obsessed by football that he will
ignore his girlfriend fainting in the crowd; in 1985, he
watches the European Cup final at Heysel on the telly,
fully aware of the deaths of Juventus fans; in January
1991, he forgets all about the Gulf War for ninety minutes; memorably, his teenage exposure to the sight of a
dead Crystal Palace fan makes him speculate not on the
mysteries of life and death but on what it would be like to
die *mid-season*.

But that's OK; it's human. What strikes us now,
paradoxically, is the superfluity of apologies in *Fever Pitch*,
because we forget what it was like – less than a decade
ago – to be shocked at somebody putting a football match
before more important matters. I remember when I was

Literary Editor on the old BBC magazine the *Listener* (which folded in 1991), we considered it post-modern naughtiness to run quasi-scholarly articles about *Crackerjack* or *Cagney and Lacey*. But in 1999, there's no shock value left in being a master of triviality, and Hornby's patent anxiety about his reader's potential disapproval is probably the most dated thing about the book.

I will tell you what's missing from *Fever Pitch*. There is no hatred in it. Being an Arsenal fan generally implies a few attendant dislikes, surely? In the film of *Fever Pitch*, for example, would a true Arsenal fan drink Holsten Pils while watching a crucial Arsenal match on the telly – when, at the time, Holsten Pils were the sponsors of Tottenham? Pah. 'No Man City fan will have a Sharp product in their home,' I was told flatly by the chap who pointed out this anomaly to me, as if the Holsten slip-up were sufficient grounds to disbelieve entirely in Hornby's enslavement to Arsenal. But much as I tried to be worried by this perceived transgression, I found that I couldn't. I think it's clever that in the whole of *Fever Pitch*, which appears to be exhaustive in its coverage of fandom, the unpleasantness of hating other clubs is virtually omitted.

And it is simply down to Hornby's character, I think. At his *Times*/Dillons event, Hornby answered a question from a fan of *High Fidelity* which raised the issue nicely.

'In *High Fidelity*,' asked the fan, 'wouldn't the record salesmen also talk about football?'

'In real life, yes,' said Hornby. 'They would be bi-lingual. They'd talk about pop music *and* football. But since the shop is in North London, I couldn't have them talk about Arsenal all the time, because I didn't want to repeat *Fever Pitch*.'

'They could support Tottenham instead,' the fan objected.

'Yes, but I'm not a good enough writer for that,' scoffed Hornby, quick as a flash. 'I'm not Dostoevsky.'

Turning the clock back on *Fever Pitch* is not the easiest of exercises. Without the publication of that book, after all, the book you are reading would not exist, and I very much doubt I would be writing about football, because no one would have dreamed of asking me. Although certain older sports writers actually snarl (I've seen them) to see their territory invaded by touchy-feely colourists who habitually can't tell you whose ball was crossed by Overmars before Bergkamp got the goal, they surely have Nick Hornby to thank for all the critics, novelists and (goddamit) women who are turning up in press boxes. Along with all those other absolutions he has handed out, Hornby said it was OK for people to react to sport, not just report it. And all of a sudden, I'm not sitting at home asking (pointlessly, as it turns out) what my characters want; I'm at St Etienne watching David Beckham get sent off against Argentina, and yelling 'What the hell's going on? This is monstrous.'

Funnily enough, what is still fresh in *Fever Pitch* is not the football. Time and Arsène Wenger have overturned Boring Arsenal; Chelsea's Stamford Bridge bears no relation to its description here; many of the football generalisations are no longer true. I particularly enjoyed the line about psychotherapy, which has been overtaken by events rather spectacularly: 'Had Willie Young ever bothered with therapy?' Hornby agonises on page 176. 'Or Peter Storey? Or Tony Adams?' But much of *Fever*

Pitch remains as fresh as paint – the excruciating episode of young Nick from Maidenhead attending Reading v Arsenal, and pretending to be a Londoner, for example; or his disquisition on how the short bigtime career of Gus Caesar disproves the idea that commitment is everything.

So we have something to thank the New Man for, back in 1991. True, he failed to duff up my boyfriend when fully within his rights, but on the bright side he sat at home and wrote *Fever Pitch*, and explained how all football sorrow takes the form of self-pity, and that if you decide to renounce the claims of adulthood, you can be a lifelong fan. 'While the details here are unique to me,' Hornby wrote in the introduction, 'I hope they will strike a chord with anyone who has found themselves drifting off, in the middle of a working day or a film or a conversation, towards a left-foot volley into a top-right corner ten or fifteen or twenty-five years ago.' Whether or not it's a good idea to encourage people to be so annoying, it's got to be admitted. *Fever Pitch*, like all great examples of autobiography, gives its readers a partial but vivid view of what it's like for all of us to be alive.

bells, smells and georgie best

PATRICK RAGGETT

Why did I not latch on to Preston North End? When I moved to Preston, a heavily Catholic town, in 1964, they were due to play West Ham in the FA Cup final. The whole school must have been fevered, yet I was oblivious. To me, there was something mythic about Manchester United that chimed with all the other myths enveloping me. Often, mid morning, Canon Finn, a burly priest given to paternal tears at the annual First Holy Communion, would arrive in class calling for two volunteers to 'do a funeral'. If chosen, I would scurry across to the church. Warm with the pleasure of missing arithmetic, I stood at the altar, in red cassock and white cotta naturally, gazing with detached interest at the weeping relatives in the front pews beside the coffin, trying to read the name plate upside down.

Earlier, the ghoulish pleasure when Canon Finn and we, his young cohorts, turned into the aisle singing the 'De Profundis' after 'greeting' the coffin as it arrived in the porch was somehow linked in my mind with the Red Devils. It seemed a part of the Catholic doctrine to support a club in which Nobby Stiles, Paddy Crerand and Bobby Charlton were reputed to take Holy Communion before each game, a club that scouted the pitches of Ireland offering footballing vocations, that played virtually every testimonial against Celtic and whose name reverberated with the death and transfiguring myth of the Busby Babes. I vividly recall my father openly expressing regret in 1966 when it was Bobby Moore, and not the posthumously deified Duncan Edwards, who lifted the Jules Rimet trophy. The bearded Georgie Best even bore a blasphemous similarity to the pictures of Christ found everywhere at home and school.

My father was a rugby fanatic. The question of taking me to Old Trafford never arose. So I lived there vicariously, hoovering up every snippet in the playground, 'Best and Charlton never speak in the dressing room,' 'I know the phone number of Mrs Aycliffe, Best's landlady.' I learned to intercept the *Daily Telegraph*. My own destiny felt bound up with United's quest for the European Cup. Listening on our radiogram to the second leg of the 1968 semi-final in the front room away from my three dismissive sisters, I almost wet myself with tension as the 1-0 lead from the first home leg was destroyed and converted to 3-1 in Real Madrid's favour. Then, miraculously, retrieved to 3-3 and a place in the final. The fact that the equaliser was scored by Bill Foulkes on a rare visit to the opposition penalty area, only increased my sense of God's involvement.

As the day of the European Cup final approached, I knew my bedtime of nine o'clock meant I would miss half the game. I was resigned. It never occurred to me to ask for extra time. I don't know why. My parents were not ogres. It was a warm May evening. After tea, I raced downstairs for a quick kick around in the road with my friends, a last rehearsal – I fancied being John Aston for the night. When I came in, my father stood in the hall. I knew playing dad was a role that made him awkward. And he knew I knew. Clearing his throat, as if having a run at a tongue twister, he said, 'You can watch it all with me if you want.' I paused. He knew what I was thinking and added with a grin, 'I don't think your sisters are interested.' Our house, like that of lots of large families, was run on rigidly democratic lines – my mother almost counted out the peas at mealtimes. Only my sisters' indifference could have stopped them from sharing this treat. But we were going to watch the match together, no sisters. This was unprecedented, this shared activity, just us. I closed the door, shutting out the rest of the house, enraptured by my father's twitching at near misses, his slippered feet jerking with the shots. I watched him watching the game. He cared.

United playing in what looked like black on our TV mystified me but did not detract from my joy at sharing that dramatic night with him. I hear now Kenneth Wolstenholme's rich tones, see John Aston, in the game of his life, tearing past his marker to the byline time after time. Best, the dark genius, rounding the keeper in extra time to give United the lead and Kidd's headed goal off the crossbar on his nineteenth birthday. The commentator's talk of atoning for Munich ten years before was literally a lifetime away for me. Instead, I marvelled at Best and Busby hugging like father and son, the huge trophy shining above Bobby Charlton's sweat blackened sleeves.

Afterwards, my father led me outside into the night. Laying his arm on my shoulder briefly, he showed me Cassiopoeia and Orion's belt. The air was still warm. I could smell the laburnum tree close by. When he pointed it out, I could make out the reddish tinge to 'Beetlejuice' in Orion's tunic. Looking heavenwards together, I felt grounded and powerful, as if this were the start of many dad–son adventures. As it happened, we never did anything like that again.

The next year, 1969, as the paper arced onto its back at the front door, I recoiled from the line announcing a 2-0 win to AC Milan in the semi-final. In the second leg, the roar of Old Trafford when Bobby Charlton's volley put them back in the tie was silenced by the referee's failure to award an equaliser after Denis Law forced the ball in. TV showed the ball clearly over the line. Matt Busby was gruffly stoic but a sense of the world's unfairness took root in me, particularly as the previous year Law had been denied a winner's medal through injury.

By 1969, the Jesuits had their teeth in me during the week and I served at St Jude's as a mercenary altar boy at weekends – avid for tips from the christened, the married and the bereaved. My form master was Fr McCulloch, a bald, ex-merchant seaman. He not only had the Jesuitical zeal for propagating the faith, but also a terrifying, fanatical obsession with football. He supported Celtic. Terrifying because a defeat for Celtic provoked punishments on Monday as arbitrary and brutal as those of any syphilitic dictator. His fanaticism consumed him. Like a deluded medieval heretic, he thought the earth was a football, the centre of the universe, with all people and matter compelled to revolve around it. As with all obsessives, he was blind to the boredom it induced in others. Often, he tested my mother's faith after Sunday lunch by inflicting cine footage of Celtic boys' teams on her and my sisters. Even I grew a bit weary of the endless, grainy replays showing the misplaced position of some scrawny youth's non-kicking foot.

But by far the worst development for me at school was that he made me his pet. I was his cherubic, fantasy son, or maybe worse in his nocturnal imaginings, immune from his bile. I remember when Celtic lost the Scottish Cup final to Aberdeen 3-1 in the early seventies. Celtic were humiliated. In his deflected rage Fr McCulloch ordered the whole row of us 'ferulas' for mocking him. This was a rubber encased whale bone shaped like a flat cosh. It stung so badly that, after getting it, the real fear was of emerging to the grinning hordes outside the head-master's office blubbing. Fr McCulloch decreed the whole row was to be punished, except, to my horror, me. Bristling with dread and anger, my classmates despised me. How I prayed to be punished, to be subsumed into the pack of baying lads. I was captain of the school team, thankfully appointed the previous year by a less partisan teacher, but now I was ostracised like some catamite coming out at a rugby player's stag night.

Fr McCulloch's ransacking influence extended into that other arena of hysteria, the soccer pitch. He was in charge of our year's school team. His blood pressure bubbled each Saturday as we maintained our record as the school's worst ever, despite Mark Lawrenson, later of Liverpool and Eire, occasionally being inserted as a ringer from the year above. Our team spirit was appalling, an indifference laced with sadism that multiplied the broken veins on Fr McCulloch's face. Any player making a mistake was verbally flayed by his team-mates, his psychic underbelly identified, the quick of his adolescent embarrassment, and ripped from him. Consequently, we went out to play on Saturdays consumed with dread anticipation, pleading coach sickness on arriving at away games only ten miles distant. Those named before kick-off as substitutes were relieved. If there had been a poisoned chalice around, we would have fought to drink from it.

For me, there was a more troubling sub-plot. Fr McCulloch would write to me in the holidays – long, rambling type-written letters splattered with exhortations, parentheses and underlinings in black ink – ordering me to attend training sessions before the new season. I would arrive to find the two of us alone in the changing room except for cine equipment. His shaking hands moved the lens while I did warm-ups and stretches, in my 'birthday suit', as he put it. This was a present I would lie awake thinking about for years later, imagining the shame of general disclosure, the whole school knowing the worst. But what was the worst? Some shadowy knowledge moved below the surface of my naivety, below the confusion caused by him exploiting his priestly authority. I sensed something sad, not sinister, underlying his voyeurism and I kept silent. On school match days, his mania to win combined with our underachieving misery to produce a density of emotion that ended not only in defeat, but included a sense of some larger failure. This did not prevent him exhorting us with a crudity that made us gawp. Yet we also felt smug that our feebleness could elicit such torrents of filth. The fact that his half-time ravings were utterly futile, and ignored, made them somehow delicious. A Jesuit half demented by celibacy and intellectual discipline was an awesome creature to behold. His language was a long way from the teachings of Ignatius Loyola. 'Your shorts should be brown not white, you wee shites, because you all shit yourselves before ye start.' Tirades like this astonished parents in earshot, but he was heedless. Piety kept them at bay while we stared at the muddy ground, knowing that his accusations of soiling ourselves were at least metaphorically true.

There were lighter moments, when his boundless love of football won him over. Then he could enchant the whole class. He strode into the room on such days, bristling and rolling his shoulders, obliterating any pretence of learning his guttural brand of Glaswegian French with a roar of 'it's the FA Cup draw at twelve noon, you little bastards!' In those moments, his antic humour, beaming at the happy clamour he unleashed, was as troubling, if we'd stopped shouting long enough to consider it, as his anger. We didn't care. A radio was produced and we gathered round. Fr McCulloch flicking his black cassock tails, rocking to and fro, as the announcer recited the slow litany of the teams in the draw.

In 1972, something miraculous happened. 'Number fourteen, Preston North End,' eliciting a collective intake of breath, 'will play number seventeen, Manchester United.' There were cracked shouts mingled with shrieks of shocked delight: a home tie against Best, Law, Charlton, no one else mattered. If the Pope and his cardinals had announced a visit, there would have been less frantic planning to get a ticket. Word got out around town that vouchers would be distributed at the next home game. Normally, North End's home gate averaged 12,000, but that day a bemused Leyton Orient took to the field before a capacity, but monumentally indifferent crowd. At dawn a few days later, after hours in the drizzle, I clutched a

West Stand ticket, a bit disappointed that juveniles were not allowed Kop tickets. We knew why. It was the era when Stretford Enders marauded like a starving medieval army. They gloried in appearing on the news, wrecking provincial towns, falling through stand roofs, pillaging everywhere. They chanted 'you're going to get your fucking heads kicked in' and the opposing fans knew it was true. On the day, the tie itself was uneventful. There was a swell of local hope when Alex Spark almost scored just after half time, before United won 2-0, just by moving through the gears when Preston tired.

The real contest took place on the Preston Kop. A line of police, their jackets flecked with gob, struggled to keep the battlers apart. Fierce fighting went on all through the game. On one side the overawed but determined locals, battling for tales in the pub at least, on the other the rabid yet clinical red hordes who had evaded the attempts at segregation. They invaded the Kop from the Town End, ominously disappearing after the kick-off, re-emerging at the opposite entrances which were open – incredible though it now seems in these post-Hillsborough days – to let latecomers in free. It was sickening, mainly because in those days it also seemed inevitable. My memory tries to linger instead on the leaps of Denis Law. I can see, like a still photo, his boots level with the shoulder blades of his former team-mate, David Sadler, as a corner came over.

Despite the violence, I left the ground enchanted with the thumping drama of it all. A rite of passage had been completed, my first Man U game and an away one at that, even if it had involved merely a ten-minute walk from home with my mother's warning (that continued well into manhood), 'Be careful crossing the roads', called out to me in front of my piss-taking friends.

Back at St Jude's, before every High Mass on Sunday mornings, we fought like baboons for totems of rank. The huge emerald-studded cross, the thurifer and the incense boat were only attained amid curses and rabbit punches. The yelping and shoving continued as the choir outside warmed up the congregation like Cliff Richard on Cup final day. I argued the merits of United with another Celtic-adoring Scot, Fr Kennedy. In the gloomy sacristy corridor, I berated him with adolescent bravado, the candles flickering, boys burning each other with wax. 'Celtic are shite compared to United, Father.'

'Away, son, ring the bell.'

'But they ARE.' I grinned as the other boys tittered at my vehemence. Fr Kennedy paused, considered the lunches my mother lavished on him, the Saturday mornings flirting with my underdressed sisters, then slid in the stiletto.

'Away, pretty boy, ring the bell.' All of us, in that dim players' tunnel, understood. As my cheeks began to burn, my heart to race and my undropped balls to retract further, he repeated himself, salaciously, slowly.

'Away, pre-tty boy, ring the bell.'

Numbly, I did, moving out among the glistening faces, carrying the cross.

Other late developers know the envy a pair of sideburns at thirteen years of age provokes, the impatient disgust for one's own hairless high-pitched body. The hairy, gravel-voiced boys knew it too, knew the power in their puberty. Those of us who lagged behind had to endure a lava-flow of 'puffda' taunts. To stem these, I did make valiant attempts to prove my heterosexuality by wooing a girl in the parish. Giddy on premature lager one Sunday at the local golf club, egged on by my downy fellow masturbators, I rang Siobhan O'Connell, whom I had lusted after for months from the altar. I knew little about her, except that her dad was rich from smashing up car batteries, but I had psyched myself for hours and, as the dialling tone whirred, imagined she had mentally rehearsed her part too.

'Hi, this is Patrick Raggett.' If not gravelly, neither was this a breathy squeal.

'Who?' she said. Undeterred, I pressed on.

'I wondered if you'd like to um – mm,' – here I realised that apart from, 'Let me wank while you strip,' I hadn't thought of anything she might agree to. 'If you'd like to see a film.'

'Well, I might. It depends who you are.' Why did it depend on that?

'Who are you?' she repeated in a voice that seemed to smile, to encourage, even though this need to identify myself was draining. Resisting the urge to bale out and hang up, I replied, 'I'm captain of the Catholic College team.' Immediately, I knew the futility of attempting to label myself in this American prom way, since she went to Edmund Campion, the vast comprehensive where eunuchs like myself would have been disembowelled long ago.

'Gaelic or soccer?'

'What?' What was going on? 'We don't play Gaelic. It's soccer, only soccer.'

'Oh. What else?'

'What else what?' Deeply miserable, I heard a giggle.

'What else can you say so I know who you are so I might want to say yes?'

Drenched in sweat I ransacked my brain for an answer. I thought of the hours I'd spent as an altar boy, sweeping the congregation for her long black hair, my hand holding the plate above her breasts at communion. Panicking, in a fog of shame and desire, I blurted, 'I read the lesson at Mass every other Sunday.' With a laugh of explosive mockery, she hung up.

My confusion towards Fr McCulloch increased the day he persuaded my parents that it was safe for him to take me to Old Trafford. The gloom of winter fingered its way through the leaded lights of our dining room, over the plates of congealing Yorkshire pudding. Persistent as a SALT treaty negotiator, he probed and prodded for his goal. I was still as limestone. My mother hesitated over the sherry trifle, loath to say anything that questioned his local infallibility, but listening to the pulse in her blood that beat a warning about her son, wondering why it was there. 'Well, I suppose if he is with you at all times, Father.' She spooned him some trifle and delivered me into his hands with a tight smile. Any misgivings I had were overwhelmed by an insomniac excitement. We were going to the derby with Manchester City.

Days before, I knew the Preston to Manchester time-table, precisely what severity of accident we could suffer, when, and at what point of the journey yet still make it to the game. Fr McCulloch was quiet and proud, an estranged father pleased after a successful fight for greater access. I was grateful. He was *loco*, but he was *in parentis* and the prize of actually going to Old Trafford was worth suffering his covert ecstasy in becoming my escort. The train journey itself was novel, the metallic, rancid odours in the overheated carriages shared with tired fathers travelling home. Victoria station was forbidding, its vast and sullen gloom. A drunk lurched at me as we stepped into the rain. I smelled his piss and shrank into my parka, suddenly homesick.

Outside the ground, it seemed every misshapen creature of God's creation seethed and jostled: my overheated imagination saw trolls come alive, returned from sealed recesses of the planet to devour pies and burgers fit to slay weaker souls. Men with pig eyes and distended bellies moved chaotically like wildebeest migrating. My heart sank as Fr McCulloch left me against the wall outside the only open pub. I thought of my dad, who never went out except to work, Asda and the church. Just then, cowed by the bestial atmosphere, I cared little for football. An age later it seemed, Fr McCulloch emerged pink-cheeked and smiling. He grasped my hand. For once I received his warm clench with gratitude. We joined the other heads bobbing to the street corner. I could see a white light arcing across the sky, as if a giant spaceship had come down for us. There was a hubbub within me as we approached the Scoreboard End. Like pilgrims hunched in the drizzle we walked towards the Stretford End. Fr McCulloch had been vague with my mother when she'd asked where we were sitting. Because we weren't sitting. If she had known that her altar boy son was to spend the evening among the demons in the 'Stretford End', it would have caused her first denial of the Church's authority. As I queued to get in, saw the surely home made stitches on the faces around me, listened to the guffaws after another Boddington's fart was expelled and got pushed into another fat arse, it all felt too much.

Dauntless as an early missionary, Fr McCulloch pushed through the turnstile with a clatter as I trailed after him. The narrow squeeze and the metal grille on the ticket collector's window made me think of a prison. Fr McCulloch looked at me, disappeared again with a terse 'Wait here, son' but this time returned with a couple of Wagon Wheels. We passed through a tunnel, up some steps, and suddenly there it was, a pitch of the most brilliant green I had ever seen, the rain glistening under the lights. There, a few yards away, a creature from the fourth dimension, his presence too strong to be true, with such fantastically hairy legs I thought, was George Best, raising an arm aloft to salute the Stretford End. Even in the warm-up, his tricks with the ball, the ethereal ease of movement, made him appear unearthly, an alien in disguise. Positioned low by the corner flag I saw little of the game. Yet how I adored the excitement generated by 63,000 voices, sensed in the heated ether.

I came away exhilarated. I had survived, flourished and grown psychically at least. Fr McCulloch took me a lot from then on. Though as much as I leapt joyfully in the seats we had moved to, rapt by some physics-defying spontaneity by Best, defenders staring after him from earth, I was discomfited by Fr McCulloch's hand gripping my thigh, his apparently spontaneous embrace and hot stale breath in my ear during the tumult after a goal. I learned to live with these momentary embarrassments. I would never have got permission to go without him.

Even with the force field of his dog collar, we could not avoid some unnerving encounters. Once, Everton were trouncing United in the League Cup 3-0 at half time. Nothing improved in the second half and Everton were cantering to an easy victory. The Stretford Enders went mad, their area only a third full by the final whistle. Outside, the streets were lined with mobs of them, scanning for anyone not wearing a red and white scarf. Even neutrals sporting no colours branded themselves as enemies by omission. We skirted the ground, past the Directors' and Players' entrance, before heading right across the concourse in front of the Scoreboard End towards the buses waiting in United Way. Directly in our path we saw a pocket of the crowd. The group looked wrong to me somehow. I pulled on Fr McCulloch's hand, seeking to veer round them but he resisted, striding straight to that bleb of malice. A pack of skinheads, in cherry Doc Martens, skinners and crombies, had two middle-aged men at bay. Incongruous, like gatecrashers, we arrived in their midst as a ghastly pause thickened the night air, each brave waiting for another to make the first rush. I felt a warm squirt of urine down my leg as one pulled out a razor. Fr McCulloch stepped right up to the biggest, shoved his big, bald, livid head into his face and roared, 'Away! You slack, snivelling, maphrotight wretch.' There was a pause, and confusion, perhaps at the wordiness, or the dog collar, like garlic to a vampire. Out of the corner of my eye, I saw one of the encircled men mouthing for air. Suddenly Fr McCulloch's head snapped sideways under a blow from behind. As his body began righting itself to the original perpendicular, it then hurtled on through another arc, his seaman's fist smacking full to the jaw of the skinhead facing him. Inwardly, I whooped at the shock frozen on the hooligan's face an instant before he fell back into his gobsmacked mates. 'Now, the lot of you, FUCK OFF.' And they did. Fr McCulloch stood panting, distracted. One of the men moved near him. 'Thank you, Father, thank you.' Fr McCulloch eyed him with an implacable fire, focus returning, sweat filming his forehead despite the cold. Then, embarrassed, fingering his collar apologetically, murmured, 'God bless, God bless you both.' We were safely on the train in the stifling compartment when he finally returned my look. 'You can see a bit better what we mean by "Soldier of Christ" now eh?' and gave a long, dry, hand-rolled fags laugh.

During school the Jesuits had a knack of conspiring to keep everyone under pressure. Many boys responded, making hormone-propelled sorties – birds against the Jesuit window panes. Almost every day, some tale spilled its drama. 'John Cherry told Fr Braden he didn't believe in God during RD and was sent home.' (RD stood for 'Religious Doctrine' although 'indoctrine' would have been more accurate.) 'Dennis O'Hara has a porno mag with real gash in it.' Each week, some boy's rebel ardour was checked by a dose of the maximum dozen ferulas.

Others were singled out and punished systematically for reasons only a psychoanalyst could have divined. Jon Lee, who came in with a gang on the train from Lytham each day, was one such. Previously, he had been notable only for his enigmatic football skills. In the yard games he was a genius with the tennis ball. But on grass with a proper ball he paled, some failure of will snuffed out his talent. Maybe that was his first mistake, or perhaps it was his mode of transport. To Fr McCulloch and a couple of the other 'football priests', Fr Braden and Fr Mahon, the 'Lytham Train' was a moving metal canister of debauchery, a vehicle for delinquents. All of us who lived locally admired the Lytham boys. Lee's second error, but one that excited awe, came after he had endured a week of punishment. As he and the rest of the Upper School filed back into class after lunch, he spat, each day without fail, in the face of a bug-eyed Fr Braden. Every day no one believed he would do it again and every day he did. Fr Braden would wipe himself, then drag Lee away for his dozen cracks. After a while, there was something weirdly fraternal about it. This went on till his parents came to take him away. He departed through a crowded but silent yard, hands like hams, Geronimo taken at last by the Yankees.

The other priests at the school, some dozen or so, were unpredictable, some days affable, more often eccentric gusting to mad. This volatility was hazardous when mixed with their pride in the school's local cup tradition. No team sent out in College colours had ever gone through its entire school life without winning at least one inter-school cup. We were to be the first. As the fifth and final campaign got going, we had a good couple of rounds. Clerical brows unfurrowed a little as we reached the semi-final. It was played not long after the World Cup match in which England had attacked Poland with everything but failed to win. It was a bright, sticky afternoon. Even before the game, nothing felt right in the sunlight. A lowering sky and drizzle would have been better. Fr McCulloch gave his team talk, his dry laughs at nothing making us edgier. As I trotted out, I understood the stakes. We played well, were even quite encouraging to each other out of respect for the occasion. The three players from Lytham redeemed themselves a bit by playing with manic passion. Yet the pattern of the match repeated the England one. We swamped their half with endless attacks but no goal came. Towards the end, we lost in the way mirthful Fate had decreed. A long clearance was hoofed towards our goal. Ged Mortimer, our goalkeeper, who a few years later would be found dead in his barracks bed in Ireland, waited to catch it first bounce. The ball landed on a divot, bouncing sideways into the gleeful path of an opponent, who scored. A few minutes later, the final whistle blew. We walked off, tired and shamefaced, fully aware of the tradition broken. None of us felt nonchalant about it. We trudged into the dressing room to strip and shower.

There was a rule that each boy had to go naked into the showers; no shorts or swimming trunks. Some cat-walked around dangling impressive machinery while others, with runtish genitalia, went around crablike. Fr McCulloch stood hands on hips as Mark Lonsdale, one of the Lytham lads, walked past in trunks. 'Och, Mark, no, take those off.' This met with a muttered 'Get fucked.' Fr McCulloch pointed at Lonsdale's arse and shouted, 'Get them off now, Lonsdale.' Lonsdale sneered. 'Why? Just so you can get a good look at it?' More sudden than the night with the skinheads, Fr McCulloch thumped him, a wide haymaker. Lonsdale's head cracked against a wall, he shook his head, wiped his mouth, then leapt on the priest. The cramped room shrank further as they wrestled, trying to get in clean punches. Having been knocked out of the Cup, our team was disbanding, Fr McCulloch had taken charge for the last time. This was some farewell. We stood transfixed for seconds, an eternity, until someone pulled Lonsdale away. That prompted others to grab Fr McCulloch and hoist him off the floor. Lonsdale looked wild, like a bolted horse. Fr McCulloch, with just a reddening above his eye, grinned at him. 'Och, I dinna think you cared, son.' Then he took off his tracksuit and joined the rest of us in the showers, offering soap around. Once dressed, we emerged together, quite surprised to see everyone else mingling, priests with mothers, men with men, hands shading the setting sun.

A by-product of Fr McCulloch's other enthusiasms was his interest in photography. When we went to Old Trafford on Saturdays, he always took his camera and a powerful telephoto lens. We sat high in the North Stand with a sidelong view of the goalmouth. Once satisfied that I understood how delicate the lenses were, he let me fire away at will. He had plenty of film and I loved bringing Best and Law closer. I tried to lip read them as they stood together in the centre circle one day against Ipswich. It was the game in which George Best scored direct from the corner opposite us. Back in Fr McCulloch's makeshift dark room off the stairs above his study, we peered and peered but couldn't see where the ball had gone. There was Best in the background, half turned sideways, watching like a distant shepherd. In the foreground, the white goalposts and a clutch of players suspended in mid air. Then in delight I spotted it. Right under the angle of the bar and post, a half sphere was visible. I had caught the moment the ball crossed the line. The images became sharper. Fr McCulloch lifted the print clear as carefully as a midwife. With a flourish, he pulled up the blind and we stood there, blinking and laughing at the happy chance of it. 'Treasure it, son, no one else in the world has that photo.' I did. I kept all the ones from that day in a large cardboard envelope under my bed. As a student a few years later, I had a holiday job in a bedding factory. One of the lads in the loading bay persuaded me to let him borrow the photos to show his mates in the pub. I had some lapse of mind and never retrieved them. I still think occasionally about putting an ad in the local paper.

When I think of the time following my last couple of years of school, the needle of memory starts to swing violently across the graph. So far as I could then tell from the TV and newspapers, Best's life went awry. The magical movement on the pitch became secondary to the story of his disappearances. The flights to Spain and the chastened returns from female sanctuary in London became as frequent as the promises of reform, soon broken. Eventually, I guess the patience of the directors and of the manager, Tommy Docherty, expired. Just before a cup tie early in 1974, dropped, Best left forever. An official announcement from the club confirmed his contract was terminated. For a few days I just could not comprehend this – as if some physical law had been transgressed. I felt my hero worship betrayed by his caprice. Time could run till kingdom come but United would never have another like him. Yet, as the world knows, almost twenty years on they did. Ryan Giggs appeared, calling forth other young acolytes blest with sublime skills and religious dedication. They combined with veterans like Bruce, Ince, Hughes and Pallister to soothe my middle-aged yearning for the League title again. I stood in my kitchen, listening on the radio to the last few minutes of Villa v Oldham. The moment Villa lost, and United were champions, I felt my boyhood self pass through me like the shadow on a hill. I had a cry and had to lie down, remembering.

Eventually, the traumas surrounding church, school and football receded, hormones did their stuff belatedly, my balls did drop. Girls became at least less openly mocking if not yet moistly enthusiastic. The ferocious joy I'd always dreamed of playing football engulfed me at university, continuing into my twenties and thirties, work's best antidote. As for Fr McCulloch, during my long vigil from childhood to early middle age waiting for the championship, on an unusually sunny day for that part of South Wales, twenty years after he had asked me to chalk 'Dad' on the back of his tracksuit before coming into shot, he married me.

the rise and fall of ruud gullit, you know

HUGO BORST and SIMON KUPER

1. Was Ruud Gullit an exceptional footballer? (1)

On 27 August 1979 I saw the second or third match of Ruud Gullit's career at the Kasteel stadium in Rotterdam. Only a thin line of Sparta fans had made their silent way down the Bilderdijkstraat. Haarlem, with Kleton, the Englishman Keith Masefield and Rudi Gullit, were not a great draw.

A lot of little old men come to watch Sparta (from 1888) and with my seventeen years I was one of the youngest people in the main stand. At Sparta football happened and happens in deathly silence. When my father lit a Northstate cigarette you could hear him from the cement Schietribune across the pitch.

We watched the match calmly. One Haarlem player was the first black footballer in ages in the Netherlands, but more than that he was the first black footballer in ages I do not remember. Sparta won 3-0, and that season Haarlem were relegated.

H.B.

2. Was Ruud Gullit an exceptional footballer? (2)

Two and a half years later, on 8 February 1982, I saw him back at the Kasteel. Still without dreadlocks, he still played for Haarlem, but he was transformed. The cool teenager carried an average team – not one of his team-mates was to become a millionaire – and was everywhere and nowhere.

In Sparta's midfield, Louis Van Gaal, later manager of Ajax and Barcelona, and Dick Advocaat, later manager of Holland and Rangers, could not hold Gullit.

'What Van Gaal made of it was nothing,' said Sparta's Welsh manager Barry Hughes afterwards.

Sparta lost 3-0. Gullit scored three marvellous goals, of which, incidentally, only one counted. 'I've had a lovely afternoon,' a relaxed Gullit told the press afterwards. Seven months later he made his debut for Holland.

H.B.

3. By what sign can one recognise powerful men?

Footballers are only interested in drinking, clothes and the size of their willies. That's not from me; it's what Karren Brady, managing director of Birmingham City, says. I would like to add to that the following: after Feyenoord played a friendly match in the 1983-84 season, I waited outside the team's changing room. Every few seconds the door would open and I would be granted a glimpse inside.

There was the captain of the Dutch national team, Bennie Wijnstekers, without any clothes on. Bennie had obviously not been at the back of the queue when they were handing out genitals.

Again the door opened. There was Johan Cruyff, naked. Gee! I knew he was the greatest of all time, but this was unbelievable.

Again the door opened. There was Ruud Gullit, naked. Good heavens! To be so good at football and also be rewarded so generously by Mother Nature.

When I told this story to the young, successful Dutch novelist Ronald Giphart he told me there was a connection.

The more powerful a man, the larger his member. Heads of state or captains of industry produce more testosterone than the average man, according to Giphart, and that hormone determines the size of the penis. There has even been small-scale research on the subject. It is thus known that conservative Republicans have larger penises than moderate Republicans and that Republicans are better endowed than Democrats, although Clinton's is not to be scoffed at, said Giphart.

The way Gullit manifests himself, in other words, betrays more than just his ambition.

H.B.

4. How much does Ruud Gullit love Nelson Mandela? And his mother?

Ruud Gullit was voted European Footballer of the Year in 1987, and when someone from the organisation asked him to whom he wanted to dedicate the Golden Ball, he is said to have answered almost instantly: my mother.

A good answer. The only right answer: where are you without your father and mother?

Someone from the organisation suggested it might have more impact if he dedicated the prize to the imprisoned Nelson Mandela. Ruud thought that was a good idea. From then on people have thought that Gullit is politically active.

H.B.

5. Was Ruud Gullit an exceptional footballer? (3)

In spring 1988, a couple of months before the European Championship, I was in Kiev to interview Valeri Lobanovski, one of the ten best football managers of the century.

Lobanovski's right-hand man, Michael Oshemkov, took me to see professor Anatoli Zelentsov, Dynamo Kiev's chief scientist. On the screen of his Commodore computer little figures walked or ran with a ball. The scientist talked about small (two or three players), medium-sized (four to six) and large (seven to eleven) group patterns. For an hour I studied dozens of combinations. It made me dizzy.

'All those hundreds of group patterns are in the heads of the Dynamo players,' Zelentsov confided. 'It's useful when you have to make decisions in tenths of seconds.'

'You can learn improvisation,' Lobanovski confirmed a couple of days later.

Anyway, after a week of hospitality, Oshemkov asked me if I could do Lobanovski and Zelentsov a favour in return. Could I obtain the height and weight of every Dutch international?

'Would it be possible to find out how quick Gullit is over 10 metres, 25, 40 and 100 metres?'

Of the quartet Rijkaard, Koeman, Van Basten and Gullit, Lobanovski thought Gullit was easily the best.

'He is clearly the worst of the four,' I replied.

'Come on. Gullit has something our players don't have,' Oshemkov translated Lobanovski.

'Yes, flair, charisma,' I said.

'We do not know the word flair in the Soviet Union,' said Oshemkov for Lobanovski. 'But it is more than charisma, flair and physical strength. Gullit does such unexpected things. His acts are unpredictable.'

For Lobanovski, Gullit, who played on intuition, was an unfathomable phenomenon.

H.B.

6. Was Ruud Gullit an exceptional footballer? (4)

It was 25 June 1988, and Holland were playing Lobanovski's USSR in the final of the European Championship. Gullit picked up the ball in midfield and began
dribbling towards the Soviet sweeper, Vagiz Khidiatulin,
on the halfway line. Suddenly he booted the ball forty
yards forward towards the corner flag. Khidiatulin had
several yards' start, but barely bothered giving chase:
knowing that Gullit would beat him to the ball, he made
straight for the penalty area instead.

Gullit was a better physical specimen than other
footballers. Like Boris Becker, Carl Lewis or Jürgen
Klinsmann, he was built to play sport. You wouldn't have
thought that he is only just average height for a Dutchman of his generation.

S.K.

7. On what subject does Ruud Gullit speak with wit and passion?

Ruud Gullit does not like dog turds. He despises the
Netherlands in general and Amsterdam in particular for
its dog turds. If he were mayor of Amsterdam he would
act decisively.

H.B.

8. Was Ruud Gullit an exceptional footballer? (5)

One morning in the late 1980s, Gullit, back in Holland on
a visit from Milan, went to train with his old club
Feyenoord.

The Feyenoord full-back Ruud Heus had made it the
pinnacle of his ambition to nutmeg the former European
Footballer of the Year. So when a five-a-side began Heus

slotted the ball through Gullit's legs and began running around him to collect it. He was interrupted by Gullit, who, according to legend, punched him drily in the face.

Whatever the truth, it shows that no one messes with Ruud Gullit.

S.K.

9. Will Ruud Gullit end up in the gutter?

He is a cheerful person and has not the slightest penchant for self-destruction. Furthermore, the Dutch business magazine *Quote* calculates that Ruud Gullit possesses capital of more than £25 million, in itself no reason to lose the way. Added to that, fate has determined that Gullit has no truck with drugs and alcohol. In 1987 he confessed the following to me: 'I don't like strong drink. But in Italy I am learning to drink wine at table. Italian wine, not French, which apparently is full of chemical rubbish. I don't like beer, and stronger stuff even less. I can't take it. It gives me a tight head. I get sick. So I don't have much choice other than soft drinks, but that makes you fat. So I drink a lot of water.'

H.B.

10. Was Ruud Gullit an exceptional footballer? (6)

It was a Thursday in November 1988, and Milan were playing Red Star Belgrade away in the European Cup. Gullit was injured, so Milan sent a private jet to bring his personal healer Ted Troost from Rotterdam to Belgrade.

Gullit played, but what really mattered to Milan was that he walked out of the tunnel with his team-mates. Just by being there he made them walk taller, cowed the opposition. Gullit recounts in his autobiography that as he came out to inspect the pitch, 'the Red Star fans went berserk, whistling, screaming and shouting at me. After five minutes of this, they stopped, and at that moment I knew I was in control of the situation.'

As his Dutch team-mate Gerald Vanenburg once said: 'Every footballer would like to look like Gullit.'

S.K.

11. Is Ruud Gullit an intellectual?

Asked about his favourite book, Ruud Gullit surprisingly replied: *The Darkroom of Damocles* by W.F. Hermans.

That answer would not get you kicked out of enlightened circles in the Netherlands. Hermans is one of the three best Dutch writers of the twentieth century and this novel is his magnum opus. That the intelligentsia nonetheless does not count Gullit as a member of its species is because he added: 'Just a shame that at the end you still don't know whether Dorbeck exists or not.'

For W.F. Hermans the essence of the novel was precisely that the question of Dorbeck's existence could not be answered.

H.B.

12. Was Ruud Gullit an exceptional footballer? (7)

Ruud Gullit was an exceptional footballer for ten months and three matches. Until August 1987, playing in the Dutch league, he was a promising footballer. With his clubs he was always knocked out of Europe before the winter, and with Holland he failed to qualify for the World Cups of 1982 and 1986 and the European Championship of 1984.

In a European Footballer of the Year election in the

early 1980s he got a vote from the German Democratic Republic. Playing for PSV, he once marched through seven AZ Alkmaar players to score a goal. But that was when Brian Clough described Dutch football as 'the Mickey Mouse League'.

Then he joined AC Milan, and in his first season he carried his team to the Italian title. A month afterwards, in June 1988, he captained the Dutch side that won the European Championship. But by then he was exhausted. He played well, but not as well as Frank Rijkaard and Marco Van Basten.

Soon after that Gullit began getting injured. In 1989 he played only three matches: the semi-final of the European Cup against Real Madrid, when he left the field on a stretcher, part of the final against Steaua Bucharest, and about twenty minutes of Finland–Holland in Helsinki, when he could barely walk, let alone run or play football, but set up the goal that took Holland to the 1990 World Cup.

The three matches were enough to place him third in the 1989 European Footballer of the Year vote. But he was injured for almost a year after Helsinki. Van Basten says Gullit was never again as good as in 1987-88.

S.K. and H.B.

13. What else can Ruud Gullit do?

An aeroplane crashes and Gullit speaks at a memorial service. He does this impressively.

H.B.

14. Is Ruud Gullit really a traitor? (1)

Ruud Gullit still leaves the Dutch guessing as to why he walked out on their national team just before the American

World Cup. A journalist with a lot of access to Gullit, Frits Barend, elaborated one theory in the magazine *Hard Gras*.

It was Frank Rijkaard's fault. The current manager of Holland, who had grown up with Gullit on the Balboa Square in Amsterdam, deserted him at the *moment suprême*.

In May 1994 Gullit found a lax atmosphere in Hotel Huis ter Duin in Noordwijk where the team was preparing for the World Cup. The closer the moment of departure came, the less faith he had in the adjusted Ajax system that he thought was doomed to fail in the damp heat of Orlando.

Rijkaard was his ally; together they discussed their feelings. Rijkaard was not to be abused as right-half, but to play in the 'axis' of the field.

On the morning after Holland–Scotland Ruud Gullit wanted to explain this to Advocaat. When Gullit asked Rijkaard at breakfast to come along and support him, Rijkaard spoke these fatal words: 'I'm not going after all. I think the manager should decide.'

I quote Frits Barend: 'Something broke in Gullit.' Perhaps it was not strong of Rijkaard not to support Gullit, but it was understandable: if Rijkaard had played in the axis then either Jonk or Wouters would have had to make way. That Rijkaard did not want that on his conscience accords with his friendly nature.

It is more probable that Ruud Gullit sensed that the other internationals were fed up with him. Although he had announced on arrival in Noordwijk that he would not interfere with anything, the story was he refused at the first practice session (after only a few minutes) to join in an exercise because he said he knew his own body better than Dick Advocaat did.

H.B.

15. Is Ruud Gullit a hero in his own country?

The Netherlands does not honour its sporting heroes. In Amsterdam they were too feckless to build a statue to Fanny Blankers-Koen. She had already had a bicycle from the city council. Wasn't that enough? The monument to the flying housewife who won four gold medals at the 1948 Olympic Games in London now stands in Rotterdam, opposite the zoo.

We don't know what to do with Gullit either. We are not even sure that he was a great footballer. The Dutch judge footballers primarily on their skill on the square inch, and Gullit in this regard was no Rijkaard, Van Basten or even Bryan Roy.

If we're not too critical we could count him as one of the best ten Dutch footballers this century – Henk Spaan, in his book *De Top 100*, ranks him ninth – but he ensures that people cannot love him unconditionally. He always makes it difficult for us. Always trouble.

The World Cup of 1990, oh boy. It is generally believed that before the tournament began he had already forced out Holland's manager, Thijs Libregts. During the tournament itself he not only quarrelled with the ball but also with the new manager (Leo Beenhakker) and a former manager (Rinus Michels), caused a newspaper war (*De Telegraaf* against *Het Algemeen Dagblad*) that unsettled the Dutch squad, and demanded the lead role in the team, when he should have played in the service of Rijkaard and Van Basten, both in peak form.

A Dutch stand-up comedian has said that football is nice because of its lack of pretensions. He says you could become a cabinet minister or a cabaret artist – people who in the back of their minds hope to give another course to history – but if you become a footballer, all you have to do is be entertaining. Gullit has seemed to never understand that message.

H.B. and S.K.

16. Is Ruud Gullit really a traitor? (2)

A few months after the 1994 World Cup, an AC Milan side, including Ruud Gullit, played Ajax in the Champions League at the Olympic Stadium in Amsterdam. People shouted that he was a Judas and produced the most piercing concert of whistles that I have ever heard in Holland.

When Gullit left Feyenoord for PSV bananas were hurled at his head and he was called a traitor. When he left PSV for Milan the same thing happened, albeit without the bananas. When Gullit left Milan for Sampdoria many in the San Siro were relieved, and when he returned from Sampdoria to Milan a year later chairman Mantovani said that Gullit had abused Sampdoria.

When he moved to Chelsea, most people (Berlusconi, coach Capello and most of the fans) seemed pleased again. Everyone remembers how he left Chelsea. If only a fraction of the things that Bates, Rix, Vialli and others said was true, one gets an unattractive picture of Gullit.

Ruud Gullit has never managed to bind people to him for long. Partings play a large role in his life. His parents divorced early. Gullit himself did so twice. And while Rinus Michels was the best manager in the world during

Euro '88, and a person for whom Gullit had high regard, they fought two years later.

H.B.

17. What does English football lack, in Ruud Gullit's view?

'Cunning,' he told the Dutch magazine *Voetbal International* in May 1996. 'In big matches you have to be clever. You have to have the will to win a free-kick near the penalty area. Falling down theatrically once. That's got nothing to do with cheating. A free-kick from twenty yards is a chance at goal. All good clubs have a specialist. For England that's Gascoigne. So you have to play towards that. But forcing free-kicks is seen as unfair in England. If you lie down you're a diver in their eyes.'

S.K.

18. Does Ruud Gullit suffer from fear of abandonment?

First you heard Beethoven's stirring ninth symphony, then you saw the cheerful faces of Desmond Lynam, Alan Hansen, Jimmy Hill and Ruud Gullit. He must have really wanted to do it, because for only £50,000 he said his piece on the BBC.

'It's a tactical game, you know.'

'He speaks good English, doesn't he?' said my mother-in-law, who had flown over from New Zealand on her broomstick and about whom I shall make absolutely no jokes here.

Gullit met a number of criteria that allowed him to analyse Euro 96 on British state television. He used to play football, just like Alan Hansen, and, you know, Gullit speaks English.

'Oh yeah, good ball, you know.'

After the opening match, England–Switzerland, I was gloomy. Gullit sat at the table looking lost, all the way on the outside, outside-right shall we say, a place he has always despised. Perhaps for that reason he analysed in something of a mumble.

No, he was not in the game at all. Hansen constantly trumped him for tactical knowledge in sweet Scottish. The former Liverpool defender kept coming in front of his man, as it were.

After the programme Gullit left the studio surrounded by four bodyguards in sunglasses. Without speaking to a single person he was chucked into a BBC car. It was an impressive spectacle, as if he were being carried off. Forever?

No! One day later Gullit was back in the studio. This time in between Lynam and Hansen. Better line-up. (Had Gullit talked to the director or to Lynam? Knowing Ruud – probably.) Gullit has always functioned better in the centre of the field, you know.

At half-time of Italy–Russia Gullit spoke these words: 'Del Piero will go off, Sacchi will put on Donadoni. You watch.' And, dammit, it happened. After the match Lynam asked why Italy had won.

'The substitution Del Piero–Donadoni was vital, you know.' Alan Hansen, who often teased Gullit, burst out laughing.

Gullit's analysis of the Italian team was, incidentally, outstanding. Better than his view of Holland. Ruud had Italianised, he knew exactly how Sacchi thought.

Furthermore, deep within him Gullit frowned upon the Dutch team, which appeared with wingers.

His greatest fear, of being put at outside-right (fear of abandonment), is probably the reason. When Alan Hansen joked at half-time of Holland–Scotland that not Gaston Taument but Gullit should be playing at outside-right, he broke out in a sweat.

'No no no no no,' shouted Gullit, as if awaking from a bad dream.

Gullit grew in the tournament. He began reducing the *you knows* by 50 per cent – as if he had begun playing more directly. One touch. He felt at ease. The result: some decent one-liners.

'A goalkeeper is a goalkeeper because he can't play football, you know.'

Ruud was just feeling good. When he was allowed to ask Gareth Southgate a question and did not seem to stop (eighty-two seconds), Lynam had to interrupt him.

'You should let him answer now, Ruud.'

Gullit laughed. He understood: television is give and take. Teamwork, you know. The head of dreadlocks rocked softly back and forth. Jesus, he was having a good time.

I thought it after the final and I still think it now. Euro 96 was the best tournament of Gullit's career. Better than 1990 or 1992. Better even than 1988!

H.B.

19. Was Ruud Gullit an exceptional footballer? (8)

In 1996 Milan fans picked their favourite AC Milan team of all time in the newspaper *Gazzetta dello Sport*. Van Basten and Nordahl were the strikers, and Rijkaard was next to Rivera in midfield. Gullit was not selected.

H.B.

20. What is Ruud Gullit like in real life?

'Jesus,' said Gullit.

I had given him the issue of *Hard Gras* that contained Frits Barend's story, and he was looking at the pictures. He stopped at one from his Haarlem days: the sixteen-year-old Gullit, with an Afro and a little moustache, standing behind a Haarlem director who was stretched out in a sort of deck chair.

'Jesus,' Gullit said again.

He turned a few pages and found a photograph of himself from the Milan era: dreadlocks, but still the same moustache.

'Jesus,' he said.

The next picture was of Frank Rijkaard, also in a Milan shirt and with exactly the same moustache.

'Jesus, Rijkaard!' said Gullit.

We were sitting in the canteen of the Chelsea training ground at Harlington, near Heathrow, and it was as if Gullit was looking at pictures of another, less stylish man. In London he had become a new Ruud Gullit.

For instance, he had recently been voted Best Dressed Man in Britain. I asked him about this. Gullit giggled – he liked the question.

'*Ach,* I don't know,' he said. 'I can wear casual, I can wear chic.' That day he was wearing a brown sweater tucked into a pair of jeans.

Gullit belongs to the select group of people who become better looking as they get older.

The new Gullit also behaved differently from the old

one. He was, to dive into his own jargon, *relaxed*. For Gullit 'relaxed' is the highest term of praise, better even than 'getting a good feeling'. He was not fighting with anyone: Hans Kraay, Thijs Libregts, Franco Baresi, Silvio Berlusconi, they were all behind him, and his sacking by Chelsea was still another year away. For a while, he had found Zen.

Because it is easy to work in a country where people respect you. Not like Holland. 'In Holland if you stick your head above the grass it gets mown off,' he told me.

'You sleep better here,' I suggested to him.

'I sleep better here,' he said.

When he arrived, he said, Chelsea had stuck him in a hotel in Slough. But one night he had hired a car and driven into London. 'And when I drove down Piccadilly, past the Ritz, I suddenly had a feeling of, "Yes! This is it!"'

Because Gullit likes *chic*.

I asked him about the differences between the Dutch, the Italians and the English.

'Well,' he said, 'in a Dutch changing-room everyone thinks he knows best. In an Italian changing-room every-one probably also thinks he knows best, but nobody dares tell the manager.'

'And in an English changing-room?' I asked.

'In an English changing-room they just have a laugh.'

Another change in Gullit: he was no longer a foot-baller. I put it to him that at practice that morning, he had not looked particularly inspired.

'I played like a turd,' said Gullit.

Playing football, he said, no longer interested him that much.

I remarked that three of his signings that season had something of Gullit the player about them: Frank Leboeuf was Gullit the libero, Gianfranco Zola the playmaker, and Gianluca Vialli the striker. 'It's as if you bought them to replace you,' I said, and Gullit immediately nodded. The same thought had occurred to him. 'Only Roberto di Matteo has things that I didn't have.'

And he told me about his plan 'to make something from nothing' at Chelsea, as he said he had at his other clubs.

I defy anyone to meet Gullit and not like him. He looks you in the eye, laughs a lot, mixes anecdotes with analysis, and gives the impression of frankness. And good footballers who are in the mood tend to make good interviews. They almost never have hangovers or low blood sugar levels nor have they woken up at 6 a.m.. And they are energetic types anyway.

By the end of the interview he had won me over. But the second I thanked him for speaking to me, he got up and began looking around for the *Daily Mail* journalist whose turn it was next. When I said goodbye, he looked at me in surprise, as if he had already forgotten who I was.

S.K.

21. What do we remember of Ruud Gullit on the pitch?

It's surprising how many different kinds of moments stick in the mind. Ruud Gullit touching a pass with the outside of his right foot, crashing a header above the keeper, driving into the top corner from thirty yards, Gullit's head motionless as he hits a forty-yard ball, Gullit tackling dwarfs.

The only thing missing are memories of Gullit being sent off. Ruud Gullit belonged on the football field; he did not lose his temper there.

S.K.

22. What is the difference between Ruud Gullit and Frank Rijkaard?

When Rijkaard came to visit Gullit in London one weekend, it took him an hour to clear customs at Heathrow. Because he was the only black man on the plane from Amsterdam, even the packets of Dutch liquorice he had brought for Gullit were searched for drugs.

It would never have happened to Gullit. He was no better a player than Rijkaard, but customs officials recognise him and kowtow.

S.K.

23. Does Ruud Gullit suffer from fear of commitment?

It must have come as a complete surprise to him. Not so much that Chelsea sacked him, but that the British papers turned on him the next day.

'You know,' Chelsea officials had whispered to journalists, 'between you and me, there was nothing else we could have done. Rudi wanted £3.6 million, and the players had had it up to here with him. Listen, I love Rudi, but . . .'

And every paper bought the line. In England, where he had been the most popular man in the country!

But Gullit is always at his best when the fish are down. At his press conference the next day he shone. Even though he had not slept all night, he spoke in complete sentences, never said 'you know', refused for once to theorise about things he knew nothing about (such as why Chelsea had sacked him, or whether his successor would make a good manager), and courteously referred to his enemies as 'Mr Colin Hutchinson' and 'Mr Luca Vialli'. When he picked his nose, he said, 'I'm sorry, I didn't want to . . .', and the 100-odd journalists burst out laughing.

At the end of the press conference Gullit laid it on too thick. He said he could now reveal that he had planned to win the league with Chelsea, and he wished Mr Luca Vialli luck in achieving this aim. Again he wished Mr Luca Vialli luck in achieving this aim. And he thanked the journalists for their intelligent articles of the past two years.

The next day he got a slightly better press, yet his reputation has never quite recovered from 12 February 1998. It turned out that Gullit was less well loved than had been assumed.

After his sacking, hundreds of Chelsea fans made for Stamford Bridge. It is conventional on these occasions for journalists to record dramatic comments from people threatening suicide and predicting an unending descent of their club à la Manchester City. That is what happened when Kenny Dalglish left Liverpool and Kevin Keegan left Newcastle.

Not this time. Tim Veck (36), a Chelsea fan from Hillingdon, Middlesex, said: 'It's a bit of a disappointment but it won't hold us back.'

Felicity Harris (52) from Mitcham, Surrey, said: 'It is a pity that Ruud had to go but I think that Vialli will do well as manager.'

Gullit had taken Chelsea to second place in the league and had won the FA Cup, but it was hard to love him because he did that so well himself.

Gullit is not a club man like Keegan, Dalglish or Cruyff. Not that there was any reason why he should have loved a club so far beneath his own status, chaired by Ken Bates and with a long tradition of racist fans. Still, it showed.

S.K.

24. Does Ruud Gullit have charisma and can he swim?

In the bar of the hotel eight German players' wives are watching their team. Their boys are 1-0 down, and at half-time a new player comes on, although 'new' is perhaps not the word.

'*Scheisse*, Lothar,' says one player's wife when she perceives Matthäus. Gullit, another attentive spectator, bursts into uncontrollable laughter. The wife colours red.

'Forgot that you lot speak German,' says Frau Babbel, or maybe it is Frau Kirsten.

Anyway, the Yugos make it 2-0. No one in the hotel bar is pleased with the goal, not even the Dutchmen who have lined up behind the German players' wives.

'If it stays like this we'll have to play the *Holländer* in the next round,' a worried Frau Babbel tells Frau Hässler.

'Trust me,' Gullit says to me, 'the Germans will come back.' A minute later it is 2-1.

'The bear is loose now, I swear. It's going to be 2-2. This is some match, isn't it? I like this, you know.'

'Are you coming swimming, Ruud?'

A long-legged blonde teenager with a covetable body. So this is she. Johan Cruyff's niece, the girl with whom

Gullit is stepping out. Estelle Cruyff spreads herself against Gullit.

'Wait a sec. The Germans are going to equalise in a moment. A quarter of an hour and I'll come out. You go ahead, darling.'

I suspect Ruud and all Dutchmen of enjoying the expectations that the Germans always meet. You want to see them come back in a match so that you can say: 'You see, Germans never give up.'

'That goal is coming,' he says in delight. 'I like this so much.'

He laughs as Ruud Gullit can. Those braces didn't do much good, I think. Orthodontists earn a lot but don't always perform commensurately.

When Bierhoff equalises to cheers from the German players' wives, Gullit bursts out laughing again.

'I told you. I swear it.'

Then he goes swimming in the Mediterranean with Estelle.

H.B.

25. How well does Ruud Gullit swim?

During the World Cup we were sharing a hotel in Juan les Pins. Almost every day on the beach in front of the hotel, there was a quiz with football questions. One afternoon the Ajax captain Danny Blind asked Alfons, a golfing friend of Gullit's, one of the trickiest quiz questions of them all.

Name the nine Dutch coaches who have won a European trophy. Alfons turned out to be an expert. He named Michels, Cruyff, Van Gaal, De Mos, Hiddink, Rijvers and, dammit, he got Wiel Coerver, Huub Stevens and the most difficult one of all, Hans Croon, who later joined the Bhagwan movement and died in a car crash.

Then Gullit said: 'Really there are nine-and-a-half.'

For a moment there is silence.

'Do you consider Chelsea's Cup-Winners' Cup to be partly yours?' I ask.

Rhetorical question.

'Oh, forget it,' says Gullit, and makes a throwaway gesture.

In all probability he would have won the cup that Vialli got. I must admit that it was very clever of Gullit to win two trophies in his first two years as a manager, but perhaps I think that because during our talks about football in Juan les Pins I was intoxicated by his charisma, even though following him in the media previously I had found him repulsive.

I see him playing in the water with Estelle. I hear Ruud laughing with his mermaid in his arms. And in the evening Ruud loyally pushes the pram and Estelle is allowed to choose nice earrings and while Estelle describes her earrings to a girlfriend in Holland by mobile phone, I talk to Gullit about Feyenoord.

'I would love to do Feyenoord in the near future. And those fans. So loyal.'

H.B.

26. Is Ruud Gullit in love with himself?

Wouldn't you be?

27. Who does Ruud Gullit support?

Soon after Gullit arrived in England in 1995, the *Daily Mirror* wrote that he was a lifelong Arsenal fan. I think we can discount that one, just as Dennis Bergkamp never supported Spurs. The Dutch are not big on supporting clubs.

But they do support Holland. When *Oranje* play a big game, three-quarters of the population watch on television. For comparison, even matches like England–Argentina in 1998 or England–West Germany in 1990 only muster about half the people in the UK.

So Holland–Brazil, World Cup semi-final, 7 July 1998 in Marseille, was a big deal. The Dutch journalists in the press box were not the only ones swearing and slamming their tables and thumping their heads on their laptops; even the French did it.

Eventually I decided it was no longer medically responsible for me to watch the game. So on the sheet with the team line-ups I began writing the home town of each member of the Dutch team.

Edwin van der Sar – Noordwijk

Frank de Boer – Grootebroek

Ronald de Boer – Grootebroek . . .

Again the sound of 60,000 people having a heart attack simultaneously.

Edgar Davids – Amsterdam

Dennis Bergkamp – Amsterdam . . .

When I had classified even the substitutes *(Ed de Goey – Gouda)*, and was still awaiting the end of extra time and our defeat on penalties, I looked around the stands.

And there, two seats away from me, suddenly descended from the ITV studio up above (even in television he shifts allegiances easily), was Ruud Gullit.

He was leaning back and his face was uncontorted. He looked relaxed.

I have no evidence for the following assertion except everything I have seen of Gullit over the last twenty years, but I suspect this: that he hoped Holland would lose.

Ruud Gullit is the only *Oranje* captain ever to pick up a prize. At the Olympic Stadium on 25 June 1988, from the chubby fingers of Helmut Kohl.

And he wanted to keep it that way. He had several friends down below – Edgar Davids, Aron Winter, Patrick Kluivert, Gullit has lots of friends – but there were others with whom he had a more complex interaction pattern.

Ronald Koeman, Holland's assistant coach, had berated him for walking out of the Dutch camp in 1994; Frank Rijkaard, another assistant coach, used to call Gullit 'Guru'; some of the young Ajax players had worn Walkmans on the team bus when they played for Holland with him. I mean, Gullit hadn't expected them to prostrate themselves before him, but surely the occasional bow . . .

And there was Dennis Bergkamp, who has never forgiven Gullit for criticising his efforts at Inter Milan. In the last game Gullit ever played, a League Cup match for Chelsea against Arsenal in February 1998, he repeatedly tried to dribble past Bergkamp and Marc Overmars from centre-back. Several times he failed.

No, my bet is that Gullit wanted Holland to lose. To use his own terminology again, he sent out negative vibes. And because he is Gullit, Holland lost.

'This is terrible for me. I feel sorry for them,' he said afterwards.

S.K.

28. Is Ruud Gullit good at doing nothing?

'Isn't twenty-eight a bit young to retire?' my sister asked me.

But I just didn't feel like it anymore. Sitting in an office in a suit under artificial lights waiting for your pension sounds more fun than it is. So I resigned from the *Financial Times*.

The problem with retiring at twenty-eight is that you have few role models except Tomas Brolin. Pondering the matter, however, I thought of two London retirees who were only slightly older than me.

One was a great English footballer of the 1970s, who lives on the top floor of a suburban tower block. Recently a friend of mine went to interview him. He knocked on his door.

No answer.

He knocked again.

After a while he began pounding rhythmically on the door.

Finally a voice called from inside: 'Chuck the money through the letterbox!'

There had to be a misunderstanding.

'But I've come to interview you,' my friend told the door. 'Don't you remember?'

'I don't care. Chuck the money through the letterbox!'

So my friend took about £50 out of his wallet and chucked it through the letterbox into the flat. However, the door remained shut. After another quarter of an hour my friend gave up and took the lift down again. There he asked an old man if he had seen the great footballer.

'Yes,' said the old man. 'He just got out of the lift on the other side of the building and ran off to the bookies.'

This footballer did not seem an appropriate role model. So I was intrigued to hear that Ruud Gullit, recently sacked by Chelsea, had been saying he felt 'relaxed'.

Gullit travelled, hung out with friends, and lay on the sofa watching TV – exactly the things I planned to do. Every now and then his agent would call Spurs and ask if there was a job coming up.

One night, watching Dutch television in Cadogan Square, Gullit had come across a documentary about sperm (which, incidentally, he took as further evidence that the Dutch are more 'relaxed' about sex than the English). He gathered from the documentary that if a woman sleeps with two men within about twenty-four hours, their sperm fight each other to reach the egg. It is a real match, complete with 'defenders' and 'attackers'.

Gullit found the programme so educational that he did not even notice the front door opening. And so a local pizza delivery man found the former Chelsea manager lying on the couch apparently watching porn from Holland.

Soon afterwards Gullit went back to work at Newcastle. That way he will never find himself legging it to the shop around the corner to score a new Italian suit.

S.K.

29. Is Ruud Gullit an exceptional manager?

Wim Kieft, who played for Holland with Gullit, wrote in the Christmas 1998 issue of the Dutch magazine *Voetbal International:* 'I had never expected that Ruud Gullit would become a manager.' Kieft said that as a player Gullit had discussed football rarely and with little thought.

He has a point. Gullit is not the type of guy to stay at

home on Friday evening watching Bayer Leverkusen – Werder Bremen – on TV.

But he is a clever manager.

On 30 August 1998, in his first match in charge of Newcastle, at home to Liverpool, Gullit made sure he started the game in the stands. He said he would not even pick the team. This meant that any hopeless humiliation for Newcastle would belong to the Dalglish era. Gullit, remember, likes 'making something of nothing'.

But he hates losing. After forty-three minutes, when Newcastle were 4-1 down thanks to Michael Owen, Gullit disappeared from the stands. 'He's already been sacked,' one fan joked.

In fact Gullit was on the way to the changing-room to sort out his team. Newcastle seemed to have decided to leave Owen unmarked and to trust in blind long punts. Gullit is not a tactical genius, but his teams do not make such basic mistakes.

And after half-time, Newcastle looked a tiny bit like a Gullit team. They played a few square balls, so that they no longer lost possession every three seconds. Robert Lee took up the Roberto di Matteo spot in front of the defence collecting loose balls, a key role in Gullit football. Owen was marked. Liverpool also grew bored, so the score stayed 4-1.

Gullit has learned the ABCs of football:

A. A good team needs more than eleven good players.

B. The most important positions are goalkeeper, centre-back, central midfield and centre-forward.

C. Good players are cheaper outside England.

D You can find out which players are good by watching foreign football on television and asking knowledgeable foreigners for advice.

E. Players who lose the ball a lot are no use no matter how hard they work.

F. A manager has to think rather than emote.

Take Gullit's main signings at Chelsea: Zola, Leboeuf, Vialli and di Matteo. None required particular genius. Vialli, Zola and di Matteo all played for Italy. Everyone knew they were good. But only Gullit signed them.

Similarly, selling Furlong was no more than common sense, although selling him for £1.5 million was arguably an act of genius.

Gullit knows less about football than Wenger or Alex Ferguson or Johan Cruyff, but he is a good manager. Gullit is good at most things. He has a good mind, a good ear for music, and he once wrote a good poem, about Holland beating West Germany in 1988. He speaks and dresses well and has found a hairstyle that suits him, and he has become a global brand like Coca-Cola.

But he was exceptional only as a footballer.

S.K.

30. Does Ruud Gullit think he is indispensable?

And one day you die. Too early or too late, never on time of course. After about four days you are buried and if you were an amiable person you are sincerely mourned and if you are lucky someone recites a poem by Jean-Pierre Rawie.

Deathbed, for instance.

What strikes me is that good and bad dead people can count on about the same number of nice words.

There is no life after death (although Gullit has said otherwise) but say you could listen in and hear the living read pieces; you wouldn't recognise yourself in them. A good thing too.

Exaggerate. You must honour dead people, if only for those who are left behind. However, I won't talk about death, but about life.

Say that life really is meant for achievement; hasn't Gullit done enough already?

I think Gullit has become a manager because he can't do without attention. We are expected to work, to be something. That all that activity leads to little or nothing does not seem to matter. We all have to become someone.

And Gullit, too, does not say: so what?

If you are a footballer you are lucky, you might say. Your life is not even half over when you are allowed to stop. I would say: disappear, buy a house near Malaga, waste your money and only do nice things.

But apparently watching TV or wandering through town or sitting on a park bench is regarded as doing nothing, even though all these are demanding activities.

Most footballers become managers.

Gullit too. Could do nothing. Should drink espresso in a grand café in Amsterdam, London or Milan, buy a suit every now and then or a sausage sandwich, take the tram to the zoo and later cook a nice meal for his wife and child, in the evening pick up Mulisch's latest novel and lying on the sofa decide to play a round of golf against Van Basten the next day.

Gullit is sometimes a victim of his ambition and vanity, but I think he can live with these weaknesses.

Van Basten has understood. He plays golf. Golf, too, is regarded as doing nothing. You should hear what people say. How he can fill his life with that. They don't understand. And Van Basten takes it seriously. Reducing his handicap as the meaning of life.

Golf has become football. Excelling in silence. No marker. No spectators. Only himself as opponent. Van Basten is starting to regard golf as being of a higher order than football. And people won't accept that either.

Anyway, Van Basten couldn't care less.

H.B.

Sections written by Hugo Borst were translated by Simon Kuper.

the contributors

The Argentinians *Adolfo Bioy Casares* and *Jorge Luis Borges* (considered the best writer never to win the Nobel Prize) collaborated on many stories together. Famously anti-football, Borges held a seminar to clash with the opening match of the 1978 World Cup in Argentina. It was not his best attended event. Neither man suspected they would ever write for *Perfect Pitch*, but Bioy Casares is well chuffed on their behalf.

Hugo Borst, Holland's best sportswriter, is under acute pressure to overcome his fear of flying: his in-laws live in New Zealand. Hugo's book *De Coolsingel bleef leeg* (about Feyenoord) is matched in Dutch football literature only by the late Nico Scheepmaker's *Cruijff, Hendrik Johannes, 1947-1984, fenomeen.* Hugo collaborated on the Gullit profile in this issue with *Simon Kuper,* co-editor of *Perfect Pitch* and author of the book *Football Against the Enemy.*

Despite attending football matches with senior Labour people for years, *Simon Buckby* has still not been given a safe parliamentary seat. He is at the *Financial Times* at least until the next election.

There was no such thing as football literature until Nick

Hornby wrote *Fever Pitch*. So there was general confusion in 1972 when *Hunter Davies* published his excellent fly-on-the-wall book about Spurs, *The Glory Game*. His piece in *Perfect Pitch* is taken from his forthcoming book *London to Loweswater*, inspired by J.B. Priestley.

Roddy Doyle is surely one of the few Booker Prize winners of recent years to support Chelsea. Very nice man, too.

Better known for her fiction, *Marguerite Duras* added to her collection of her own erotic writing when she met Michel Platini and impressed him with her understanding of his job. Sadly she did not live to see France win the World Cup.

Simon Inglis suffers from a peculiar addiction that drives him to write books about football grounds. His next book is about culture, history, politics and (there's no two ways of saying this) football grounds.

The Brazilian *Rita Lee* is a woman of many talents, but she will forever be remembered for her single *Lanza Perfumi* everywhere west of the Atlantic.

Emma Lindsey almost wrote a book about the Jamaican football team. Fortunately it ended up as a long piece in *Perfect Pitch* instead. Her bizarre family history could be her next subject. Toying with the idea of becoming a lawyer and author of the best-written briefs in Chancery Lane.

Patrick Raggett has come home from Hong Kong and given

up the law in order to become a journalist. His article in this issue is only the second unsolicited manuscript ever published by *Perfect Pitch*.

Amy Raphael is, as she often points out, not the daughter of Frederic Raphael. This does not matter, because Amy can write perfectly well by herself. Divides her time between *Esquire* and *Perfect Pitch*.

Daniel Samper's love affair with football has led him to write the biography of one Faustino Asprilla, as well as landing him in no end of trouble, as he tells *Perfect Pitch* readers. He lives in Spain having exiled himself from his native Colombia, leaving the running of the country to his brother, ex-president Ernesto.

Eamonn Sweeney is Irish, as may become apparent from his article in this issue. His first novel *Waiting for the Healer* brought 'both Nick Hornby and Roddy Doyle to mind', said the *Guardian*. Hardest contributor to get hold of in the history of *Perfect Pitch*.

D.J. Taylor has just written a Thackeray biography. For *Perfect Pitch*, this workaholic Orwell nut has produced the essay that Orwell should have written. Every issue the editors thank God on their bare knees that D.J. Taylor exists.

Lynne Truss is, in a sense, a creation of Nick Hornby. It is due to him that she began writing about football for *The Times*, and in her second contribution to *Perfect Pitch* she unravels his legacy.

Jorge Valdano is a natural born writer who also happened to achieve substantial recognition as a footballer for both Argentina and Real Madrid. He managed Real, Tenerife and Valencia before retiring. But he has asked whether it would be possible to manage a Premier League team without speaking English. See the Ruud Gullit piece.